STUDIES IN MODERN EUROPEAN LITERATURE
AND THOUGHT

General Editor:
ERICH HELLER
Professor of German
in the University College of Swansea

PAUL VALÉRY

PAUL VALÉRY

THE MIND IN THE MIRROR

BY

ELIZABETH SEWELL

BOWES & BOWES
CAMBRIDGE

First published in 1952 in the Series
Studies in Modern European Literature and Thought
by Bowes & Bowes Publishers Limited, Cambridge

Printed in the Netherlands
by Joh. Enschedé en Zonen, Haarlem

I

Magic mirror on the wall,
Who is the fairest one of all?

There are some people who cannot pass a looking-glass without
a slight disturbance in their imagination. It is not just vanity,
masculine or feminine. It is something more, partly a sense of a
hidden significance in the mirror's inverted images, for a mirror
is not neutral as is a picture or a piece of wall; partly, also, a
sense of reassurance at the sight of one's own image, a twisting of
Descartes' maxim into 'I reflect, therefore I am.' It is to some
extent a game, half serious as most games are, as Kipling knew
when he described Queen Elizabeth's sidling progress towards
her mirror:

> Backwards and forwards and sideways did she pass,
> Making up her mind to face the cruel looking-glass.

Those who share this slight mania will understand, while those
who do not must accept that it is so with certain minds and be
patient for the time being.

Mirrors occur here and there in literature, just as they occur
here and there in an ordinary house. One remembers the one in
the Epistle of St James, where the observer kept forgetting what
he looked like; there is Tommie Trot, the man of law, who

> Sold his bed and lay on straw,
> Sold the straw and lay on grass
> To buy his wife a looking-glass.

Hamlet was himself 'the glass of fashion'; the Lady of Shalott
owned one,

> a mirror clear
> That hangs before her all the year.

If, however, one were to come upon a house lined with mirrors,
mirrors in every room, hanging on every wall and facing all the
staircases (and such houses exist), one would begin to wonder,
and would not regard that as an ordinary house any more. The
same thing is true of literature. It is a curious and interesting
fact that mirrors become increasingly frequent in literature towards the end of the nineteenth century. I do not want to insist
on this, or indeed on anything in this brief study of Paul Valéry
who himself said of the mind, 'Je suis rapide ou rien': I am rapid
or nothing worth (*Monsieur Teste*). None the less, the collection
of mirrors in literature at this time seems unusually large, par-

ticularly in the work of three writers, Stéphane Mallarmé, Paul Valéry and Lewis Carroll. Carroll sends his small heroine through the looking-glass into some new country of the mind. One could almost say of Mallarmé's *Hérodiade* that it too takes place in a mirror; this also is the setting for the sonnet 'Ses purs ongles . . .' where someone is 'défunte nue en le miroir' with the Seven Stars of the night sky for background. Then there is Mallarmé himself, sitting, as he admitted in a letter to a close friend, in front of a mirror as he wrote, to make sure that he would not disappear into that nothingness which during the writing of *Hérodiade* his soul had seen and shuddered at.

Valéry adds to this in his turn, in prose and poetry. The prose works, as we shall see, are full of references to mirrors. There are mirrors in *La Jeune Parque*, his major poem:

> Un miroir de la mer
> Se lève . . .[1]

There is one in *Ébauche d'un Serpent*–'Orgueil de mon sombre miroir'–from the collection *Charmes*. There is one in *Amphion* and one in *Sémiramis*, the two verse dramas for music which Valéry wrote in the thirties. Finally, there are no less than three poetical works on the subject of Narcissus, who fell in love with his own face mirrored in the lake. The first, *Narcisse Parle*, is an early poem, and appears in the *Album de Vers Anciens;* the second, *Fragment du Narcisse*, is in *Charmes*, and the third, *Cantate du Narcisse*, is dated 1938.

It is as if, during the second half of the nineteenth century, literature were turning itself into a *Galerie des Glaces*–the French word being so much more expressive than the English one, conveying as it does the suggestion of ice as well as glass, the 'froid féroce' which Valéry's Faust discovers at the highest point of abstract thought in the mind, 'essential solitude, the extreme of the rarefaction of Being' (*Le Solitaire*, Scene II, *Mon Faust*). It is in this cold, lonely, mirror-haunted stretch of time that Valéry belongs.

Born in 1871, he began writing very early, and by the time he met and made friends with Pierre Louÿs, another young writer, in 1890, he was in a position to formulate his literary creed: 'Never again will my artistic ideal abandon itself to the hazards of inspiration' (Letter to Louÿs, dated June 2nd, 1890). For the next three years Valéry was writing the poems which were later collected and published as the *Album de Vers Anciens*. It was in 1891 that he made the acquaintance of Mallarmé, and, as was more or less inevitable in a young writer of his turn of mind, came very much under the influence of that extraordinary individual, then not far off the premature end of his life, most of his

[1] English translations of passages quoted in the text will be found on pages 55-59.

poetry–so difficult and so unlike anyone else's–already written, still holding round him the young *élite* of the literary world. Mallarmé's influence on Valéry was, however, more personal than poetic. The younger man was confirmed by the older in that passion for precision, analysis, consciously constructed mental perfection, which they share, but it did not lead him to poetry. On the contrary, by 1892 he had already decided to give up the writing of poetry, and from this year till 1912 he worked, so he tells us, entirely for himself, without thought of publication, though some of his notes were published later in the *Variété* and *Tel Quel* series. What was he studying? Science and mathematics for the most part so far as one can tell, though as a means to an end, working out his own mental forms so as to be able to think in them (*Cahier B* 1910, *Tel Quel I*). A few prose works date from this time. *Introduction à la Méthode de Léonard de Vinci* appeared in 1894, *Monsieur Teste* (*teste* is the old French form of *tête*, meaning *head*) in 1895, both important since both are self-analyses of the mind; *Une Conquête Méthodique*, Valéry's first excursion into political writing, in 1896. There is no poetry for twenty years, until 1917 saw the publication of *La Jeune Parque*.

This is Valéry's longest and perhaps his best-known poem; it bears the distinction of being known as the most obscure poem in the whole of French literature, and brought its writer immediate fame, and controversy. The *Album de Vers Anciens*, already mentioned, appeared in 1920. Two years later a second collection of poetry came out, *Charmes*, which contains *Le Cimetière Marin*, *Ébauche d'un Serpent*, *La Pythie*, *Cantique des Colonnes* and other of his more famous poems. From then until his death in 1945 there is a steady output of works in prose, works on architecture (*Eupalinos*), on art (*Pièces sur l'Art*), on the dance (*L'Âme et la Danse*), on all three at once in *Degas Danse Dessin*; there are works on contemporary Europe such as *Regards sur le Monde Actuel*, collections of essays, thoughts, conversations, on these and other subjects, *Variété I-V*, *L'Idée Fixe*, *Mélange*, *Tel Quel I* and *II*, *Mauvaises Pensées*, and a small output of verse and poetic drama.

When Valéry was born Charles Baudelaire had been four years dead, he who had raised French poetry to new heights and whose work, sombre though it was, was illuminated by a strange unearthly light,

> Dont les yeux mortels, en leur splendeur entière,
> Ne sont que des miroirs obscurcis et plaintifs.

Valéry is of the same poetic generation as Yeats and Rilke, and is often to be found classed in works of literary history and criticism as a symbolist, the faithful disciple of Mallarmé, whose poetic methods he is supposed to have extended both in time and in scope. The label of 'symbolism' is no more useful than such labels usually are, and there is little to be gained by calling Valéry a symbolist if by that is meant an adherent of an ill-defined poetic group existing in France at the end of the last century. The word 'symbol' is in any case misleading. It suggests that a poet is putting down something for something else, using a certain image which is a direct substitute for whatever it is that he is talking about, a rose to stand for Love, for example. This in turn is likely to suggest that the symbols and the poem need interpreting; and indeed Valéry has been much interpreted. His obscurity is not of this kind, however, and it is important to sweep the symbols off the floor before we begin, lest there should be any misunderstanding about the nature of Valéry's work, or of the work that confronts us in trying to appreciate it, with the mirror as starting point.

There is much to be said for Roger Fry's view that in a world of symbolists there are only two people fundamentally opposed to symbols, the artist and the man of science, both of whom are concerned with construction. Valéry had claims to being both, but his chief preoccupation was mental construction, and this means that anyone who is going to try to meet his mind must try to construct something as well, with the help of such science and poetry as the mind can muster. There is no definition but by construction, as Valéry says (*Instants, Mélange*). It is useless to try to interpret any poet's work, by symbols or any other literary technique; all we can do is to attempt to build something and hope that in so doing we may a little conform our minds to the shape of his.

What was the shape of Valéry's mind? He was continually trying to discover that himself, not because it was his own mind but because he was fascinated by the ways of thought in general, of which, as he says, we know so little. He was a poet and a precise and rigorous thinker, but at the same time he was always watching himself making poetry, watching his mind thinking and making a form and structure out of its thoughts. Valéry's mind watches itself in the mirror.

This is like Carroll, whose *Looking-Glass* is at once Nonsense and a commentary on Nonsense. It is like Mallarmé, whose poetry is so pure that it is about poetry and nothing else at all, a form commenting on a form, the content irrelevant. These three minds have something in common here which the mirror may betoken, for them and for us. It is not to be thought of as merely an obsession with self, which the mirror might suggest, a per-petual introspection. There may be more to it than that, and one comes nearer to it by remembering the Latin word for a mirror, *speculum*. Is there some connection between *speculum* and speculation, the mirror and the exercise of the intellect? The words suggest it, and again one remembers the curious ambi-guity of the word 'reflection', which can mean either the face in the mirror or the workings of the mind. This, too, is not a point to be laboured; but it is worth considering whether these mirror-haunted poets were not at the same time speculative intellects, minds who could construct networks of thought, or networks of words that would emerge as poetry, and who saw no division between the two exercises. The work of Carroll, himself an expert in mathematics and logic, is all about the mind; Mallarmé thought more about his art than perhaps any poet has done before or since, and has left us his thoughts, looking-glass fashion, half-veiled in his prose which is supposed to be about something, and openly in his poetry which is not intended to have a subject at all. Valéry denies categorically the distinction between poetry and abstract thought: 'I could not bear (from 1892 on) that the poetic state should be set in opposition to the full and sustained activity of the intellect' (*Mémoires d'un Poème*, *Variété V*).

It is as if, during this period, the spirit of speculation–if one may use such a phrase–was appearing in unexpected places. Speculation or speculative thought is not to be regarded as an empty theorizing about dull abstracts. It is by its very nature constructive, for the mind in speculation is trying to build up a framework of thoughts, and if it has done its job well, the framework may serve some purpose; or it may not. It cannot, being purely mental, build anything tangible, and it is this that may make its operation a little difficult to grasp. It can only build a form, a structure or pattern in the mind, something like a mental house of cards, a cobweb, a network of thoughts that hold together, the important thing being the holding together, the logic, and not the subject matter or the conclusions. Like dialectic, the art of argument, it is best thought of as a game, and perhaps the highest game the mind can play.

The Schoolmen of the Middle Ages knew about it, but we lost it with the Renaissance and the Reformation, and by 1850 nobody was being taught to play the game of thought, any more than they are nowadays, and poets and thinkers were taking themselves seriously, and separately. But the spirit of speculation, like another such, bloweth where it listeth, and the later nineteenth century saw a number of developments that have perhaps some bearing on this: the growth of symbolic logic as the basis of all pure mathematics, that superlative game; a great development in the practice and theory of chess, the noblest of the games of thought; and, lastly, the renewal of speculation in the minds of the poets. In mathematics and logic, the playthings are technical symbols; in chess they are chessmen; but the poet plays with words, and that is his advantage and disadvantage, for pure mathematics, symbolic logic and chess are closed books to those who do not have an innate appetite for them, but words are common property, and the game the poets play, whether they are thinking webs of thought or spinning webs of words, is accessible to anyone. The game itself, if it is to be played and appreciated, needs only the readiness to play and be played with, and the capacity to enjoy construction for its own sake, without useful and practical ends.

Although logic and mathematics and chess still flourish, poetry and hard thinking are in danger of becoming separated again. Mallarmé and Valéry are dead, with no visible heirs; in England the only one who took this tradition over from Carroll was G. K. Chesterton, but he lacked the intellectual discipline to carry it through to perfection, either in thought or poetry, and since then the game has lapsed. But it is essential that it be revived, for poetry and thought will sicken if they cannot go on playing with one another. We no longer, alas, study the Scholastics, and so have forgotten how to think, forgotten that science and art belong together, that art is an intellectual virtue and that wisdom and games are to be pursued for their own sake. With heads untrained and idle we are too solemn to appreciate a transcendental game such as Mallarmé plays, or too lazy to join in. We think comfortably that hard thought is beyond our powers, and forget that mathematics and logic produced the Alices, to confound us.

Valéry is perhaps the best player, the most clear and conscious mind of them all. 'As much consciousness as possible' (*Mémoires d'un Poème, Variété V*) was his device for poetry, the union of poetic enthusiasm and precise directed thought, the mind watching the mind, inverted simulacrum in the mirror. The nature of that mirror of the mind, what beauty and horror and strangeness it may reveal, will be our subject here. In one sense it will be Valéry's mind, but in another it will be the mirror of any mind, no matter its personality and thought-content, 'research into the general conditions of all thought, irrespective of its content' (ibid.) which was what Valéry himself was pursuing. If Valéry was thinking about thinking, that is what we are going to have to do. It is perhaps worth noticing at this stage that Aristotle says in his *Metaphysics* that thinking about thinking must be the characteristic activity of the mind of God.

II

The image of the chessboard is present to their minds as if in a mirror.

TAINE

Judging by the range of subjects which Valéry deals with in his writing, one might think that his mind was a peculiarly far-reaching one, capable of being interested in almost anything. In one sense this is true. Valéry was a great believer in universality, but indirectly. He was interested in everything because he was interested only in one. 'As soon as the mind is involved, everything is involved' (*Cours de Poétique, Variété V*); but Valéry was interested in so much only because he was passionately interested in the mind. In one sense his range was very narrow, if his mind was not. He says himself: 'I can see for my part that the selfsame subject, and even the selfsame words, could be taken up again and again, indefinitely, and could occupy the whole of a lifetime' (*Littérature, Tel Quel I*). He seems almost to suffer, in his own words, from an *idée fixe;* but in the book with that title he defines the *idée fixe* in terms of movement. 'An idea cannot be fixed. The only thing that can be fixed (if anything can be) is something that is not an idea. An idea is an alteration–or rather, a mode of alteration–indeed the most discontinuous mode of alteration.' Valéry's *idée fixe* is the movement and play of thought.

In 1894 we find him writing of 'the possibility, almost the necessity, of a generalised play of thought' in the *Introduction à la Méthode de Léonard de Vinci*. In his *Note et Digression* on that work he speaks of 'that Intellectual Comedy which has not yet found its poet, and which in my view would be even more precious than the *Comédie Humaine*, than the *Divine Comedy* itself.' That was in 1919. To this he adds later: 'I have taken as my programme in life the increase of consciousness in the operations of the mind, applying this to poetry'; this was said in a lecture dated 1928.[1] Time counts for nothing in this preoccupation. It is 'le jeu de la pensée' which is in question, that game which Carroll saw in terms of cards and chess, Mallarmé in terms of dice in *Un Coup de Dés*. If the game is one which deals with mental relations, you can begin it very young. Indeed, it is interesting that only in fields of mental relations–mathematics, music and chess–do infant prodigies occur. The prodigy will have to grow up, but the game will stay the same all through the player's life. This explains why so many themes that are characteristic of the later Valéry are already contained in the Leonardo essay and in *Monsieur Teste*, both early works.

Valéry himself has been identified with each of these figures by certain critics, who maintain that he never developed beyond this stage, and who see in the recurrence of these themes throughout his life a sign of arrested development and spiritual sterility. This is nonsense. It is this never-ending attention to the game of thought which makes his work supremely interesting and unlike any other. His writings on some definite subject, essays on politics, on Paris and France and French civilization, on literary figures, on impressions of travel, poems about women, trees, the sea–all these, one feels, could have been written by almost any

[1] Delivered to 'La Société Française de Philosophie', and published in *Vues*, La Table Ronde, 1948, under the title of *La Création Artistique*.

cultured and talented Frenchman. It is his repetition that is his most interesting feature. Valéry denies that the mind, in its most essential being as mind, can ever repeat itself: 'To take up an idea again, consciously, is to renew it, to modify, enrich, simplify or destroy that idea' (*Mémoires d'un Poème*, *Variété V*). There is and must be, however, repetition in matters of form; indeed Valéry maintains that form is in essence bound up with repetition (*Littérature*, *Tel Quel I*). In the nature of his own repetitions lies the form of Valéry's system of thinking; and that is as it should be, since he had a passion for form.

This may look like the beginnings of a division of Valéry's work into form and content, that well-worn and occasionally useful artifice of literary criticism which attempts to divide the subject-matter so that the mind may the more readily play with it, separating and distinguishing two limited concepts where in reality there is only a whole–defining, in fact. Something defined is something separated from one's own mind and therefore manipulable. 'Everything which we can define distinguishes itself immediately from the mind which produced it, and goes into opposition. In the same moment it becomes for the mind the equivalent of a material on which the mind can operate or an instrument by which it can operate' (*Cours de Poétique*, *Variété V*). But in the case of Valéry and his work, this distinction between form and content has to be abandoned. 'They set up *form* and *content* in opposition to one another . . . and do not see that *what they call the content is only impure* (that is to say, *muddled*) *form*' (*Je Disais à Stéphane Mallarmé*, *Variété III*).

This may be easier to grasp if we think of it in terms of drawing or painting. Of subjects in this branch of art, Valéry says: 'The visible world is a perpetual stimulus: everything awakens or nourishes the instinct to appropriate to oneself the outline or the modelling of the thing *which the observer's glance constructs*' (*Suite du Précédent*, *Degas Danse Dessin*). Here content has become form, but this in its turn is not to be separated from the activity of the mind. This comes out even more clearly in a remark of Degas which Valéry reports a little later in the same work, 'drawing is not the form, it is the way of seeing the form.'

Here we are back to the mirror again, to Monsieur Teste saying in *La Soirée* . . . 'I am existing and seeing myself; seeing myself see myself, and so on'–'Je suis étant et me voyant, me voyant me voir.' This is one of the places where the mirror image we are using may justify itself, for without some such help it is difficult to visualize this situation. We have had to give up the distinction between form and content, and between form and mind; but to abandon distinctions is to make thinking not easier but harder. Forms of thought, ways of thinking, mental systems, are what Valéry is interested in, and these are in his mind, and indeed in any mind that thinks consciously. Thought is not something outside of and entirely separate from the mind; but neither is the reflection in a mirror. One knows that there is in reality only one face and not two; but none the less an image of that one face appears before one's eyes, and so can be studied. The unity but the seeming doubleness of mind and thought can be perhaps imagined in the same way. After all, one cannot imagine without an image.

The inability to separate mind and thought at this stage has one advantage, however: it poses at once the problem of what one might call reciprocal action in any thinking. Clearly, a mind may construct its thoughts, may make them into something, a book perhaps, or a poem. But at the same time that mind is undergoing its work as well as creating it, being constructed as well as constructing. 'The work modifies the author', as Valéry remarks (*Autres Rhumbs, Tel Quel II*), and this is what interests him. He owned that he had the mania of loving nothing about works but their process of generation (*Note et Digression, Variété*), and that he was always more attentive to the formation or fabrication of works than to the works themselves (*Poésie et Pensée Abstraite, Variété V*).

The idea of transformation, which is implicit here, plays an important part in Valéry's thinking. (One might notice that the term 'transformation' itself, which Valéry frequently uses, is a technical term in mathematics.) In *L'Idée Fixe* he says, 'An idea is a means or a signal of transformation, which operates to a greater or lesser degree on the whole being.' But minds and ideas transform one another. 'Anyone who has just completed a long work . . . experiences the terrible humiliation of feeling himself becoming the child of his own work, borrowing unmistakable features from it, resemblances, peculiarities, a limit, a mirror' (*Autres Rhumbs, Tel Quel II*). Just so, in *Through the Looking-Glass*, Alice is at one and the same time the player of the game of chess and a substitute for the White Pawn, Lily, thus becoming a pawn herself, i.e. someone else's plaything. The same notion is in Valéry too. In the beginning of the *Note et Digression* he likens thinking to a game of chess, and adds elsewhere, 'The artist would count for very little if he were not the plaything of what he is making' (*Mémoires d'un Poème, Variété V*).

It is unusual, this concentration on mind and work while they are still one, preferring their interplay to the finished production, whatever that might be–system of thought, work of art, poem. It follows that one might expect Valéry to prefer his own work in just that state; and so he does. This man who spent four years working on *La Jeune Parque*, of which he made two hundred and fifty typed drafts, whose prose is as polished and symmetrical as the pillars in his own *Cantique des Colonnes*, whose name stands for the most exacting rigour in the use of language, he it is who says, 'If I were to write, I would infinitely rather write something weak, in full consciousness and in complete lucidity, than give birth to a masterpiece in a state of trance' (*Lettre sur Mallarmé, Variété II*). We shall come back to this question of consciousness and unconsciousness, but for the moment it is enough to notice the complete disregard of nearly all that is usually understood by perfection in literature. It looks as if, by reason of his lack of interest in the finished work, he would have to devote himself to the half-finished, the only partially ordered, the imperfect. He has his own definition of perfection, however: 'Perfection is *work*' (*Littérature, Tel Quel II*); and what at first sight seems a commonplace acquires a new force. It is in the cross- and counter-play of mind and production that end and perfection lie. The actual ending of a work, its abandonment by its author as finished, seemed to him little more than chance. 'A poem is never finished–it is always an accident which puts an end to it, that is to say, which gives it to the public' (ibid.). Thought, like dialectic or the Alices, has no end; the player stops playing, that is all.

In view of this it is perhaps strange that Valéry should have produced and published any written works at all. I think he was himself aware of this inconsistency, for he always seems a little embarrassed when speaking of his own literary productions and goes out of his way to emphasize the fact that all his prose works which are not just collections of fragments were commissioned, the result not of internal pressure but of editorial demand. (See the foreword to the joint edition of *Eupalinos, L'Âme et la Danse* and *Dialogue de l'Arbre*, for instance, or the description of the origin of *Une Conquête Méthodique* given in *Souvenir Actuel, Regards sur le Monde Actuel*.) *La Jeune Parque* itself was the indirect result of a request made by André Gide and the publisher Gallimard.

'Writing is distasteful to me' he says in *Cahier B* 1910, *Tel Quel I*–'écrire me répugne.' Valéry has been accused of affectation on this account, and indeed the attitude does seem strange in one who made literature his career; but if we are right so far, it is a quite genuine attitude on Valéry's part. A mind that loved the construction of mental systems would be bound to feel some uneasiness at having to use words which end the mobility and potentiality of the thought by making it actual, fixing it, in a published work at least, for ever–if the work lasts that long. Perhaps the only explanation is that of Pooh-Bah, which covers so many things in human existence: 'It revolts me but I do it.' Valéry explains that the construction of purely abstract systems which never had to stand the test of practice seemed to him to savour unpleasantly of facility. He would, he says, have preferred 'arts that reproduce nothing', such as music. (The whole problem is discussed in *Mémoires d'un Poème, Variété V*.) Language as a means of construction was for him an object of suspicion, but words were all he had, as must be so with minds that have not received a training in purer languages such as music or algebra. He curses words in good round terms, calling them impure, monstrous, incoherent, unreliable, trombones, parrots, idols; but they were none the less his only medium. All he could do was, in his thought and prose, to exercise a rigorous selection in the words used, and to turn to the most difficult and complicated construction with words that is possible, namely poetry. As he admits, however, poetry is not a private cult, it is Literature (ibid.); and so, by a sort of logic, Valéry's own poems saw the light.

Given his interests, however–his passion for thought forming in the mind and forming the mind–his poetry is likely to be of a very particular and personal kind. Critics who have said that his work is like that of Mallarmé must have run the two together in a common obscurity, like two trains running into one another in a fog. Valéry speaks of Mallarmé, in the *Lettre sur Mallarmé* in *Variété II*, as 'a mind so different from my own', and he is surely right. Valéry's best poetry is like no one else's because he was attempting something new. His poems were being made not so much for their own sake as for the sake of their effect upon his mind. That is why he called them exercises, a word that stands in the dedication to André Gide of *La Jeune Parque* which is perhaps his masterpiece. This too has been held to be false humility on Valéry's part, but it is merely exactness.

This partly is what he means when he says that the life of the intelligence is an incomparable lyric universe (*Descartes*, *Variété IV*); that there might exist 'a poetry of the wonders and the emotions of the intellect (which I have dreamed about all my life)' (*L'Homme et la Coquille*, *Variété V*). If his aim was not content but form, not the product of a mind so much as its exercise, this may account both for his obscurity and for the astonishing effect his work has on the reader's thought. If Valéry's work was a mirror, for himself and others, that does not mean that the one looking into the mirror is passive. In *Au Sujet d'*EURÉKA, from *Variété*, Valéry says, 'A woman modifies herself in front of her mirror.' So does Valéry; and we are compelled to do likewise, caught up as we are within the framework of his own reflection.

III

> . . . *From mirror after mirror,*
> *No vanity's displayed.*
> *I'm looking for the face I had*
> *Before the world was made.*
> W. B. YEATS

In the section called *Instants* in *Mélange* there is a little passage headed *Monologue ou Dialogue?* It seems to be a conversation inside a mind; there is an 'I' and there is a 'Thou', each opposed to other, as the face reflected in a mirror is opposed, or opposite, to its counterpart. Carroll's Alice, we may remember, 'was very fond of pretending to be two people', and she was always talking to herself. So the question arises: monologue or dialogue?

The mind seems capable of dividing itself into two, in a number of ways, and we say 'I am talking to myself'–a curious phrase when one looks at it. In the same way we speak of inner conflict, of a personality divided against itself and needing reintegration, of not being at peace with oneself. All these phrases suggest a Tweedledum and Tweedledee existence in the mind, following perhaps the rule of those gentlemen: 'Let's fight till six and then have dinner.' The problem has invaded literature, with Goethe's Faust who complained that two souls lodged in his breast, and it had a good run in the nineteenth century with the *Doppelgänger* of the Romantics and Stevenson's Jekyll and Hyde. Literary statements of it, however, are liable to be misleading. It is easier to stick to our own image, the face in the looking-glass. Monologue or dialogue, two or one? It seems either or both, a question that has no answer, and that is its importance, because it is one of the ways to start thinking about the mind and its workings, as Valéry saw it.

It is interesting to notice how frequently Valéry in his prose employs the form of the dialogue. *Eupalinos* is a dialogue. *L'Âme et la Danse* admits three characters but could well be called a Socratic dialogue. The *Dialogue de l'Arbre* speaks for itself. *L'Idée Fixe* is the record of a long conversation between two people. Three short dialogues, *Orgueil pour Orgueil, Colloque dans un Être, Socrate et son Médecin*, are included in *Mélange*. Even Monsieur Teste has his interlocutor whom we meet in *La Soirée avec Monsieur Teste*. But as soon as one realizes how much dialogue there is in Valéry's prose, something else follows: his major poems, *La Jeune Parque, Ébauche d'un Serpent, La Pythie*, the first two Narcissus poems, *Le Cimetière Marin*, all take the form of monologue. It looks as if Valéry's mind at times carried on a dialogue with itself (indeed he says so in the foreword to *Mon Faust*), but at other times lost its double identity. In him, the first of these two conditions produced the prose, the second the poetry; or perhaps cause and effect worked the other way round.

These two forms of mental activity, dialogue and monologue, will provide us with what we need, a way of dividing up Valéry's work for closer examination. It is very unsatisfactory, particularly with a man of Valéry's turn of mind, to attempt a chronological division, or a rigid classification into prose, plays, poetry and so on. What I propose to do is to take one theme, an aspect of the mind's working, and let that run its course through the prose into the poetry. The progression will generally be that way round, from two into one and from dialectic into equilibrium. We shall deal in time with each of the monologue poems just mentioned, but not as the starting point for analysis, rather as the answer, or a possible answer, to the questions which the prose works will set, 'mirrors in which the consequences and the perspectives of his thoughts are drawn out to infinity' (*N, Mauvaises Pensées*). As befits the consistency of our own imagery, we will start, or rather end this chapter, with the Narcissus poems. With the later poems we shall be able to turn our attention to outward as well as inward subjects. For the present, however, we have to stay by the mirror and see how Valéry looks at thought or at his own mind, observing it in his own glass in order to find out 'by meditations and confrontations that the one who looks at himself in the mirror and the one whom he sees there have certain common and indivisible properties' (*A, Mauvaises Pensées*). This, he says, is one of the definitions to which the whole of philosophy can be reduced; not that Valéry, or this investigation, has any concern with professional philosophy.

This hovering between dialogue and monologue, between two and one in the mind, is in one way unsatisfactory, because it is mysterious. The mind undoubtedly has its mystery, but in matters of the intellect and intellectual construction one may not seek for mystery nor remain content with it, particularly when one is dealing with Valéry, for whom words such as 'genius', 'mystery', 'profound', '*Variété*', were signs of impotence of thought (*Note et Digression, Variété*). It is, however, one of the strange things about the mind–and Valéry, I suspect, knew it–that extreme precision generates its own mystery. He speaks in *L'Idée Fixe* of physicists who have carried analysis so far that they reach an order which resembles nothing. A little later in the same work he throws doubt on the adequacy of the phrase 'One and one make two.' Our difficulty is that we are faced, in Valéry, with that very problem, the apparent equivalence in the mind of two and one, a straightforward contradiction. But the contradiction is no accident; 'our contradictions are the evidence and the effect of the activity of our thought' (*Instants, Mélange*). It is necessary to be clear about this, because contradiction in our subject-matter does not mean that we are allowed to lapse into a muddle in our heads. The best way to begin will be to look at Valéry's distinction between the singleness and doubleness of one mind, one being.

The activity of thought, the personality, the 'I' or self, all these are for Valéry complexities of one sort or another. Of thought he says that it 'is the thing which is at the same time something other than oneself; and which is so always' (*Analecta, Tel Quel II*). Of personality: 'It is certain that we are woven of relationships, and very odd ones at that . . . Therein the whole of the personality resides' (*L'Idée Fixe*). Of the self: 'I! . . . that is to say, the Thou the most constant, the most obedient, the first to awaken and the last to bed' (*Cahier B* 1910, *Tel Quel I*). But this is not the whole story; the mind may start in complexity, but there is a working towards unity, as the passage in *Mélange* called *Souvenir* suggests; 'I regarded, if you will, thought as an unknown, and by as many approximations as were needful I advanced towards "it".'

The progress in the mind from two to one is set out most clearly in the *Note et Digression* to the Leonardo essay in *Variété*. The passage is too long to quote in full, but it is an attempt to answer the question: What is the nature of the inalterability of the mind, through all its own activity, the action of the universe upon it, the slow decay of the organism to which it is attached? The answer is given in these words, 'Ce n'est que cette conscience seule, à l'état le plus abstrait', consciousness in its most abstract form. Valéry makes a distinction between consciousness and the personality which, he says, 'is only a thing, mutable and accidental beside this most naked *self*... only a secondary psychological divinity, which inhabits our mirror and answers to our name.' He goes on to say that it is the hidden but essential work of the greatest minds to define themselves, not in terms of the personality but in those of 'this self to which no words can be applied, which has no name and no history, which is no more perceptible and no less real than the centre of mass of a ring or of a planetary system.' This is for Valéry the goal to be attained, where the mind 'feels itself to be pure consciousness: there cannot be two.' It is in a sense the goal of all knowledge and study. 'A truly *precise* mind can understand only itself, in certain states' (*Choses Tues, Tel Quel I*).

But just because the mind is, in Valéry's way of thinking, simple in this state, it is unknowable. Aquinas would put this in one way, saying that the human mind can know only the complex and that simple things are notified by negations.[1] Valéry puts it another way, saying, 'There are no names for the things amongst which one is really alone' (*Note et Digression, Variété*). Here is too much of a oneness; you can do nothing with it. It is the face without the mirror, 'a mirror where one looks at oneself, and which gives one the desire to talk to oneself' (*Moralités, Tel Quel I*). Valéry is using that particular phrase as a commentary on the strange text in the Psalms, *Dixit Dominus Domino meo*, the Lord said unto my lord. He comments on it again in *A, Mauvaises Pensées*, saying this time, 'My spirit thinks of my spirit which is its equal–of its equal which is its essence. Its essence is the difference between like and like.' As if in a mirror, the mind has to look at itself, to talk to itself, to construct problems for itself to solve, to oppose itself. Valéry gives it as one of the characteristic properties of mankind that we can divide our-

---

[1] *Summa Theologica*, Part I, Q. 3, Art. 3, and Q. 33, Art. 4.

selves against ourselves, that we have the faculty of producing an
inner antagonism against ourselves. 'Nous avons *l'âme opposable*'
(*M, Mauvaises Pensées*).

If therefore the mind must seek for its own inner unity, it must
also be able to work in the opposite direction, turn itself from
two into one and from one into two; it must foster its ability to
complicate itself so that it may think the better. And we move
with it, from monologue to dialogue.

There is a *Dialogue de Nuit* in *P, Mauvaises Pensées*, which runs
like this:

    – Who is there?
    – I !
    – Who is *I*?
    – Thou.
    And that is the awakening–the Thou and the I.

This conversation is in some sort prolonged, or more fully
reported, in the *Colloque dans un Être* (Colloquy in a Being), in
Mélange. Here the voices in the dialogue are called A and B, both
being in the mind at the moment of waking, A compelling the
dreaming and contented B to come to life. Awakening and life
are stated in terms of order, analysis, differentiation, thought
active upon itself, doubled activities for the one mind, and A's
ideal for B is 'You are going to differ from yourself.'

At this point we, who are thinking about this change from
monologue to dialogue which comes with the increase of control
of the mind over itself, must be careful not to over-simplify. We
still have to find out more about it, with Valéry's help; but as
soon as one starts thinking of the mind as divided in some way
one runs the risk of getting involved with such alien divisions as
the Freudian, for instance, or the division into intellect and
imagination, or perhaps that between the intellectual and the
corporeal powers. These dualisms, the stock-in-trade of psy-
chology and philosophy, will be no help here. So far we have
this to go on: that oneness of some sort in the mind (though pos-
sibly the means of unification may differ in each case) seems to
reside in the inner and most intimate and essential consciousness; in the sleeping self; in the self when active in the field of
art, which Valéry describes as 'a complete action which should
bear witness, even in the most futile production, to possession of
the fullness of the antagonistic powers which we have in us'
(*Mémoires d'un Poème, Variété V*). No ready-made halvings of the
mind can help us here. All we can be sure of is that, according to
Valéry, an increase in complexity and a moving from singleness
to doubleness of activity in the mind is the necessary accompani-
ment, or result, of an increase in consciousness. It is worth noting
how, in *La Soirée avec Monsieur Teste*, Teste as he drops off to sleep

lapses from dialogue into monologue. And with the mention of Teste we come to our chief sources here, Teste being one and Leonardo the other.

Valéry's own mind is to be found in the picture he gives of each of these. He admits it in the second case: 'I confess that I found no better expedient than to attribute to the unfortunate Leonardo my own agitations . . . I dared to consider myself under his name' (*Note et Digression*). Teste is a slightly different case, for he is pure intellect embodied, and this inevitably makes him something of a monster. Teste is an extreme where Valéry is more central, but they differ (as Teste differs from all minds regarded solely as such) only in degree and not in kind. Valéry has been accused of arrogance in this connection, both for his concentration on his own self, Narcissus-fashion, and for certain remarks such as the opening one of *Monsieur Teste*; 'La bêtise n'est pas mon fort'–stupidity is not my strong suit. If this is self-love, however, it is of a strange kind: 'We have to learn not to believe our thought because it is *our* thought. On the contrary, we have to hold it in and to regard it with greater suspicion, because it is *our* thought' (*A, Mauvaises Pensées*). Valéry deals with the case himself, in the *Note et Digression*. 'What other than ourselves can answer when we call up a *spirit*? One can only find such in oneself. It is our own functioning, and that *alone*, which can teach us anything about everything.' What then can we learn, from Leonardo and Teste and Valéry, of the functioning of any mind, its single and double states and its way of providing itself with a mirror and so giving itself itself as an object of observation?

The Leonardo essay (included in *Variété*) is called, with an affectionate remembrance of Descartes, *Introduction à la Méthode de Léonard de Vinci*, and so it is a definition of a method that we have to look for. Valéry begins by recalling the enormously varied interests and activities of Leonardo, art, science, speculation, philosophy, engineering, aeronautics, stage design, ballistics, architecture, anatomy, pell-mell; and he goes on to suggest that out of this diversity and disorder of interests and curiosities the great mind has first to unify not its subject-matter but itself. This is the first indication: 'It (i.c. the intelligence) applies itself to forming a decisive image. With a violence which depends on its breadth and its lucidity, it ends by reconquering its own unity.' But observe the nature of that unity as stated here: a definition of the self, if one thinks about it, is scarcely what one would think of as unity. To have reached a definition of oneself would mean that one could think clearly about oneself, i.e. had set up the conditions not for monologue but for clear and precise dialogue. This becomes a little clearer when Valéry says later on, 'The consciousness of the thoughts one has, in so far as they are thoughts, is to recognize this kind of equality or homogeneity; . . . the method consists in stirring them up, in observing them with precision, in seeking what they imply.'

It seems that Valéry is saying that the thinking mind's only chance of unity is a carefully defined doubleness or reciprocal action. Once this is achieved, however, all sorts of doubled and redoubled possibilities arise. They are not very clearly worked out in the Leonardo essay. Universality, however, is claimed for the method, with Leonardo's own magnificent boast, *facil cosa e farsi universale!*–it is easy to make oneself universal. One unity achieved is the denial of the distinction between art and science for a mind that has perfected the method in question. This is interesting, and there is more to follow, for it looks as if this method in the mind–the definition of the mind by itself so that it may work with itself, in familiarity with its own doubleness and its image in its own mirror–may immediately abolish a number of false dualisms, such as the science-art division. (It is significant that the Scholastics who perfected the art of dialectic, a game for two minds or two voices in one mind, also understood that science and art were one and not two.) Valéry sets down in the *Note et Digression* other dualisms which vanish with this method: 'I felt that this master of his media, this possessor of drawing, of images, of mathematics, had found the central attitude from which, working outwards, the enterprises of knowledge and the operations of art are equally possible; happy exchanges between analysis and action singularly probable.' Here the 'entreprises de la connaissance' and the 'opérations de l'art' have become one–which looks like the union of *poésie* and *pensée abstraite* again; so have analysis and action–or are these two sets of pairs really one and the same thing, since conscious thought is analysis, and art is certainly action, being concerned, as St Thomas says, with the making of external things?[1]

Valéry, speaking of the brain, calls it in the Leonardo essay a monstrous creature, the strange animal which has spun myriads of pure relations between so many forms. This fits Monsieur Teste rather well, as indeed it should; and the interesting thing about him is that although at first sight he looks so different from Leonardo, he works on just the same principles.

In the *Dialogue ou nouveau Fragment relatif à Monsieur Teste* we find this passage, a development of what Valéry had already said about Leonardo's method: 'He had one advantage over everybody which he had given himself: that of possessing a suitable idea of himself; and in each of his thoughts there entered another Monsieur Teste, a familiar being, simplified, united to the real one at each of his points. He had, in fine, substituted for the vague suspicion of the self . . . an imaginary being, well defined, a carefully determined or educated self, as reliable as an

1 *Summa Theologica*, Part I-II, Q. 34, Art. 1.

instrument, as sensitive as an animal, and compatible with all things, as is man himself.' The passage goes on to speak of Teste 'armé de sa propre image'–armed with his own image, a wonderful phrase, as if the duplication in the mirror were a protection, as perhaps it is.

The effect is simplicity, of a sort. In *Pour un Portrait de Monsieur Teste* we read, 'Teste enters, and strikes everyone present by his "simplicity".' The inverted commas round the word are not there for nothing; but Teste has achieved some of the same simplicities as Leonardo, the uniting of art and science, for instance. They were all one for this mind: 'One of Teste's manias . . . was to want to preserve art–*Ars*–while exterminating the illusions of artist and author' (*Pour un Portrait*); 'ancient desire . . . to reconstruct everything in pure materials; nothing but definite elements . . . nothing but conquered forms, and no vagueness' (*Extraits du Log-Book de Monsieur Teste*). Here too the distinction between analysis and action is, in theory, null: 'If this man had changed the object of his enclosed meditations, if he had turned the regulated power of his mind against the world, nothing would have resisted him' (*La Soirée avec Monsieur Teste*).

Thus these two figures, as Valéry drew them, tell us a little–and that little not easy–of what it means to define oneself as a thinking mind, to hold up a mirror to the mind's face and, in seeing that doubleness, to attain a greater unity. The process is carried to its logical conclusion in a little extract from Teste's Log-Book, 'So direct is my vision, so pure my sensation . . . so accomplished my science that I penetrate myself from the extremity of the world to my silent speech; . . . I *am* myself, I respond to myself, I am my own reflections and repercussions, I vibrate in an infinity of mirrors–I am of glass.' This is the extreme and the end of the process, even for Teste, who has taken the method of Leonardo as far as it can be taken. But Teste adds something more, something capital that brings us to another famous dualism, and to the Narcissus poems where we shall finish. In *La Soirée* Teste has been talking about numbers, the Stock Exchange, money. Then, without warning, comes this small and telling paragraph: 'All at once he stopped talking. He was in pain.' Monsieur Teste is subject to pain, and with that notion comes the whole question of the mind and the body, and their astonishing connection.

Later in the Teste collection, in *Pour un Portrait*, we find the remark: 'At the end of the mind, the body. But at the end of the body, the mind.' The theme is taken up elsewhere, as in *N*, *Mauvaises Pensées*, where it is suggested that without the points of contact between the body of a thinking man and his chair, his thought would degenerate into dream or disappear altogether. Here the Narcissus poems come in. We have been using the mirror image for a mind examining itself, but Narcissus in the myth is a body looking at its own bodily reflection and worshipping its lovely face; and that face is flesh and blood as well as the spirit that informs it.

> O forme obéissante à mes yeux opposée!

This is the first of the Narcissus poems, the *Narcisse Parle* of the *Album de Vers Anciens*. It sets out the circumstances without elaborating them, though the choice of the subject-matter is interesting in itself. With the second, however, the *Fragment du Narcisse* in *Charmes*, there is a development. Obviously I cannot give any idea of the three poems in detail. They should be read one after another; and already with the second the growth of the theme will be apparent, in such phrases as:

> Je suis seul! . . .
> Seul! mais encor celui qui s'approche de soi.

The ambiguity of it all, the singleness with the doubleness, is there; the echoed words (as in the original myth), the endlessness of the obsession and its isolation,

> Nulle des nymphes, nulle amie, ne m'attire
> Comme tu fais sur l'onde, inépuisable Moi!

the confounding of body and mind,

> Voir, ô merveille, voir! ma bouche nuancée
> Trahir . . . peindre sur l'onde une fleur de pensée,
> Et quels événements étinceler dans l'œil!

the hymn to the body and its beauty,

> O mon bien souverain, cher corps, je n'ai que toi!

But towards the end there is also this line,

> O mon corps, mon cher corps, temple qui me sépares
> De ma divinité,

for the body is a separation, just as the reflection is split from its original by the mirror,

> Cher trésor d'un miroir qui partage le monde!

The mirror can impart the world and its treasure only by dividing, and there is a great sadness at the end.

With the last of the series, the *Cantate du Narcisse*, other voices come in, those of the nymphs whose love is offered to Narcissus only to be rejected, and those of the uncertain and shadowy gods. All the themes of the last Narcissus are taken up again, but at the end there is a new note; or perhaps it is only the development of what was implicit in the story all along. At the end of the legend, Narcissus was changed into a flower, and here, too, some such fate is foreshadowed for Valéry's Narcissus, some form of dissolution and death for the being who loves none but himself. The final stage direction reads 'Il disparaît'–he disappears.

It is not only Narcissus who ends so. 'Marche funèbre de la pensée', funeral march of thought, is the last phrase in *Monsieur Teste*, where Teste is meditating upon his death, a thing he was apparently given to doing, since at the end of Madame Émilie Teste's letter we find him murmuring '*Doctement mourir*'–to die learnedly. Teste had said earlier, 'And I myself! which I tear to pieces and which I nourish with its own substance chewed over and over, the only food it can grow on!' (*Extraits du Log-Book*). Extremity of thought consumes itself, having only itself to feed on, and in the end it will die of it. 'The thinker is a man in his death-throes', Teste says, in some way separated already from the body and the world around him (*Fin de Monsieur Teste*). For the body that Narcissus loves, the body that casts the image in the looking-glass, the body that sustains the thought, is mortal. '"Farewell"', says the dying man to the mirror held out to him, "we shall never see one another again"' (*D, Mauvaises Pensées*).

In *Mélange* under the heading *Avec Soi Seul* there is a little passage in prose called *Narcisse*. It says:

Is it not to think of death to look at oneself in a mirror? Does one not see there one's perishable part? Immortal looks upon mortal. A mirror takes us out of our skin, out of our face.
Nothing resists its double.

Valéry does not speculate on the connection or disconnection of body and spirit, in life and death. In *Note et Digression*, it is true, he mentions Leonardo's view that death is a disaster for the *soul*, reaching home to the soul's dearest work by destroying the architecture which it had made for itself to live in; and goes on to talk of the dogma of the Catholic Church on the resurrection of the body. But Valéry has no such certainty.

L'âme, l'âme aux yeux noirs, touche aux ténèbres mêmes,
Elle se fait immense et ne rencontre rien . . .
Entre la mort et soi, quel regard est le sien!

The night falls over Narcissus' pool, and what use is the mind if, the face gone from the mirror, it has nothing but darkness in which to lose itself? The body is solid and well-defined, the mind can limit and define itself, and each can behold the other in the mirror; but death dissolves the body and in some sense unlimits the soul. 'Une chose inimaginable', according to Monsieur Teste; but the last word is with the poetry, which says what the prose said but in its own way and perhaps better, as we shall find all the way through. They say poetry is compact of images—but here Valéry goes one further, for his image of the end of life and thought is an absence of an image. In Valéry's mirror there is no spectre, no form of death, angelic or sepulchral. There is only a darkened stretch of water, the pool untenanted, the mirror dead; and one holds one's breath a moment.

IV

Tell them, if any should enquire
How this thing came to pass,
I saw the darkness of the moon
Within my looking-glass.

THE SUICIDE

Valéry in his *Lettre sur les Mythes, Variété II*, employs a phrase from St John, but with a difference, beginning his own Valeryan gospel with 'In the beginning was the Fable.' Since Valéry is a commentator upon St John, we might do worse than borrow a figure from St John, the Apocalypse this time, as a commentary on this next stage of our enquiry into Valéry. We have indeed, as Valéry says, to begin with an image, a figure (I hesitate in the circumstances to use the term 'fable'), for we are coming now to what are perhaps the less rational and controllable elements in the mind, as Valéry saw them, and these may best be approached by figures. It is as though a walk were no longer possible but only the dance, as God (so some fables tell) danced in the beginning of the world, and priests and people agree in measured and ritual movement as if in answer and almost as a means of comprehension. Valéry would understand such a measure, for he knew that 'our only resources for dealing with our interior material and self are of the order of symbolism and magic' (*Littérature, Tel Quel I*).

St John calls up before us the figure of a woman upon whose forehead was written the name MYSTERY. It would please Valéry that mystery should be a woman, and that her superscription, as St John gives it, should run on: THE MOTHER OF HARLOTS AND ABOMINATIONS OF THE EARTH. He hated mystery. Its name was for him one of the words which cloaked mental impotence; and that is interesting, for he himself defines hatred of something as follows: 'Hatred and repulsion (*a priori*) are frequently signs that one lacks the organs, faculties or energies

25

which would permit the exploitation, utilisation or consumption, etc., of the things for which one feels hatred. I am not sure of being able to overcome you, turn you to my account, annul you; therefore I hate you, I suppress you in my mind' (*Choses Tues, Tel Quel I*). Hatred of something is an affirmation of that something's existence.

In *A, Mauvaises Pensées*, Valéry has a run of paragraphs on mystery. 'What is called the mystery of the world or the mystery of life' he begins, 'is no more mysterious in itself than the inability of the eyes to look at the back of the man they belong to . . . How should a man without a mirror picture his own face?' Give the mind its mirror so that it may see its own countenance, and the mystery will vanish.

It seems to be the same story over again; but it is not, for Valéry gives himself away. The mirror, that image of the conscious mind, can show so much and no more. Not every face is shown in it, and Valéry himself goes on, in that same passage, from talking about mirrors to talking about the dark face of the moon, which we cannot see and never shall. There is no mystery, he says, that is just how things are. But the admission creeps in elsewhere: 'All things are strange' (*Moralités, Tel Quel I*), and the human face can be as strange and unfamiliar as any of them. 'Our face is as strange to us as it is to other people'; only a remnant of its possibilities reaches us, and that only from mirrors (*Petites Études, Mélange*). So the mirror, too, leaves room for mystery and the dark side of the moon; and the moon is, in myth and fable, a woman. A woman, a moon in the night sky, a ritual mystery: it sounds an irrational muddle, but it will serve our purpose, for we come now to that division of the mind–if division it be–into rational and irrational, and the latter will be our main concern.

We have already seen a little, and shall see more, of his unwillingness to accept mystery; but even he cannot consistently deny the existence of this shadow side of the mind. Even his clear and logical spirit from time to time looked into the mirror and saw there another face, that of a woman,

> Pâle, profondément mordue

who says of herself

> Morte, errante et lune à jamais.

Those lines are from *La Pythie* in *Charmes*, the poem with which we shall end this chapter and in which we may hope to learn something of Valéry's mind in this metamorphosis. *La Pythie* is the pythoness, the priestess of the oracle who in her intermittent trances emits not her own sayings but those of the god. Mention of her occurs here and there in Valéry's prose as well, and we will turn to the prose first and knit up the problem which the poem must solve.

Teste in his Log-Book says, 'Between the clear I and the dark I (*Moi clair et Moi trouble*) . . . there exist ancient hatreds and ancient compromises.' Valéry is at first sight more concerned with the antagonism between these two, *Moi clair* and *Moi trouble*, the day and the night side of the mind, the clear, controlled, constructive intelligence against the wild, the inspired, the chance-ridden. Nietzsche called this division Apollo and Dionysus, and Valéry makes use of this in the *Note et Digression* in *Variété*. He says there, of Leonardo, 'This Apollo ravished me to the highest degree of which I was capable. What could be more seductive than a god who repulses mystery, who does not base his power upon the clouding of our senses, who does not address his marvels to the most obscure, the most tender, the most sinister piece of ourselves? . . . Never did Dionysus have an enemy more deliberate, more pure, or armed with more light than this hero.'

Valéry sees three principal manifestations of the Dionysus in the mind: dreams, passion and inspiration. He would reject them all, as products of chance which the creating action of the artist must sort out and transform and oppose if they are to be brought under the mind's law. It is not merely a question of ordering them, but of making them personal, for to Valéry each of these forms of enthusiasm seems alien, a possession by some external and overwhelming force which is a violation of the individual rights of the spirit.

Of dreams Valéry has a good deal to say. One of the speakers in *L'Idée Fixe* says of them, 'I have reflected for a long time on these curious compositions', and that may well hold good for Valéry himself. They are discussed in the Note to *La Crise de L'Esprit* in *Variété*; nightmare is discussed and defined in *Lettre sur les Mythes* in *Variété II*, and the theme is taken up in the following chapter, *Études*, and reappears in sections *D* and *L* of *Mauvaises Pensées* and in various places in *Tel Quel I* and *II*. The relations between dream and poetry are discussed in *Au Sujet d'Adonis* (*Variété*), though with careful limitation, as for instance in such remarks as 'He who speaks of exactitude and style is invoking the opposite of dream'. The two meet again in *Poésie et Pensée Abstraite* (*Variété V*), and again are likened and distinguished: 'Neither dreams nor day-dreams are necessarily poetic.' Their alien nature is clearly brought out in the *Dialogue de l'Arbre*, where Tityre maintains that he cannot be the author of his own dreams.

The same thing is true, in Valéry's mind, of inspiration. In an essay on Mallarmé published in *Le Point* in 1944 and reprinted in *Vues* he says, 'There was, and is, a mystery of inspiration,

27

which is the name given to the spontaneous formation in someone of statements or of ideas which appear to him to be wonders of which he feels himself by nature incapable. He is therefore assisted.' He says elsewhere that such a notion ought to be unbearable to a poet; 'to be a transmission agent is a humiliating notion' (*Autres Rhumbs, Tel Quel II*). It is true of passion as well. Teste says, 'Loving and hating–*seem* to me to be matters of chance' (*Extraits du Log-Book*), and 'Consider the emotions as follies, debilities, useless things, imbecilities, imperfections . . . Something in us, or in me, revolts against the inventive power the soul has over the mind' (*Quelques Pensées de Monsieur Teste*). Love is compared with dream in *Autres Rhumbs, Tel Quel II*, and with magic in *G, Mauvaises Pensées*, and in *D* in the latter work it is said of the emotions, 'Nothing iş more foreign–hostile even'.

Socrates in *Eupalinos* says that love, wine and 'the astonishing action of those vapours inhaled by the pythoness' set the mind beside itself, but adds that they have no connection with the subject which he and Phèdre are discussing–the construction of beauty. It is to this that Valéry constantly returns, for the creation of beauty, particularly under the form of poetry, is for him the touchstone by which these enthusiasms may be tested and found wanting. Dream is not poetry, he tells us in *Autour de Corot, Pièces sur l'Art*; and again: 'The pythoness could not dictate a poem. Only a line–that is to say a unit–and then another. This goddess of the continuum is incapable of continuity' (*Rhumbs, Tel Quel II*). Wherever the pythoness appears she is the image of the irrational, the product of hazard. In a footnote to *Analecta* in the same volume she typifies spontaneity as against deliberate reflection. In *Littérature, Tel Quel I*, she is a badge of shame ('Blush to be the pythoness'), like the MYSTERY in the Apocalypse.

Valéry would be glad to deny her, this unmanageable feminine dweller in deeps and darkness. Whenever he can he denies her her atmosphere and necessary conditions. The nymph in the *Cantate du Narcisse* who unites womanhood and passion and darkness,

L'excès de ma tendresse aux ténèbres se tient,

is rejected. The morning and the new sunlight are greeted with something approaching worship. 'Upon waking, how sweet the light and how lovely this living blue! The word "Pure" opens my lips. Such is the name that I give thee . . . This azure is a Certainty. This sun appearing . . . makes his entry and mounts up like a judge, calling pale error before his tribunal; he condemns dreams; he scatters the beliefs of night, annuls the judgments of fear; he reassures or threatens all things in the mind' (*Autres Rhumbs, Tel Quel II*). Like the sun, 'consciousness comes out of the twilight' (*Choses Tues, Tel Quel I*). If the pythoness is the moon and darkness, the sun is the image of the conscious mind. Carroll uses the same image in the *Walrus and the Carpenter*, where the sun has come out in the middle of the night, offending the sulky moon by doing so but making a noble effort to keep at bay that dark dreamy feminine side of things to which Carroll, in his work and his person, was as hostile as Valéry was.

Besides darkness, Valéry abhors depth. 'Only superficial things can manage not to be insignificant', he says; 'that which is deep has neither sense nor consequence . . . That which is deep is (by definition) that which is distant from cognition' (*Analecta*, *Tel Quel II*). He despises Pascal for his fear of the dark spaces of the universe and says as much in *Variation sur une 'Pensée'* in *Variété*, and elsewhere. The gods in the *Cantate du Narcisse* have the same two characteristics, depth and darkness, applied to them.

> Ma Fontaine lucide, ils n'ont qu'un fleuve obscur
> Pour témoin ténébreux de leur toute-puissance.

Impurity is for Valéry the most striking thing about religion (*Divinités, Mélange*), and in a discussion on it he says, in *Choses Tues, Tel Quel I*, 'Do not hope to hook me in muddy water.' The final word lies with the mirror: 'What does it matter if this pool is forty centimetres or four thousand metres deep? It is its brightness that delights us' (*Rhumbs, Tel Quel II*).

Here are *Moi clair* and *Moi trouble* confronting one another again. But remember that between them there are not only ancient hatreds but also ancient arrangements and compromises. The resistance of the one to the other is in itself a relationship between them. Valéry reserves the right to struggle: 'I invoke only that hazard which is the basic stuff of all minds; and then, an obstinate labouring which is *against* that very hazard' (*Autres Rhumbs*, ibid.). This however, is not the whole story. Because Valéry knows that and has set out the other side he has been accused of self-contradiction; but he is merely reproducing the contradictions of life itself, for this is once again the problem we were looking at earlier, the apparent equivalence of two and one. There are not two minds, two selves. *Moi clair* and *Moi trouble* are both *Moi*, the one self. The strange face in the looking-glass, the dark side of the moon, is our own. There is no final distinction, as the last prose comment on the pythoness shows:

> I reflect . . .
> Is that anything very different from that practice which consisted (as it always will) in consulting the 'spirits'?
> Waiting in front of a table, a pack of cards, an idol, or a pythoness moaning in her sleep, or else in front of that which one calls 'oneself' . . .
>
> (*A, Mauvaises Pensées*).

Reflection is conscious thought, and here Valéry identifies it with the pythoness, who stands for the exact contrary.

Chance, divination, possession by the divine and arbitrary, discontinuity, falsehood, muddled ideas, all these which Valéry detests play a capital part, as he admits (*N, Mauvaises Pensées*), in the working of the mind; 'error and impotence function.' The mind is chance, knowledge is chance (*Cahier B* 1910, *Tel Quel I*), chance is more myself than I myself (*P, Mauvaises Pensées*). Chance gave birth to Teste, to the cold implacable intellect, 'as with all the world. All the mentality that he has or had comes to him from this fact' (*Pour un Portrait de Monsieur Teste*). The distinction between thought and dreaming is equally uncertain. We reach this by degrees, seeing first that ordinary, i.e. undirected, thought is the dream of a waking sleeper (*Introduction à la Méthode de Léonard de Vinci, Variété*). But we move on from here, and the more far-reaching equation is formulated in *P, Mauvaises Pensées*: 'When I am thinking, I am dreaming.' A dreaming Reason is spoken of in *L'Âme et la Danse*, and in an article on science in the collection *Vues* Valéry compares dreams to scientific thinking, a form of thought which holds its head very high and would not be flattered by the comparison.

If this be true, then the conditions which govern dreams, the chance, the inescapable toils of the dream imagery, the possession as if by some alien power, cannot be very different from those which govern the working of the intelligence. Valéry admits this. The apparently alien nature of our ideas is touched on in the essay *Fluctuations sur la Liberté* in *Regards sur le Monde Actuel*: '*My* ideas come to *me*, *I* know not how and *I* know not whence.' The idea of thought as external violence is there too. 'Thought is brutal–unsparing. What more brutal than a thought?' (*Autres Rhumbs, Tel Quel II*). 'One must exert or suffer violence if one is to see better or differently' (*Cahier B* 1910, *Tel Quel I*).

This leads straight on to the inescapable conclusion, and so back to the pythoness again, but to her of the poem this time. In *D, Mauvaises Pensées*, we read, 'O self, it is not you that finds your idea; on the contrary, it is an idea that finds you and adopts you.' Valéry, who hates and fears inspiration, admits in the end that our ideas no less than our dreams and passions are a sort of possession. Teste knew it all along, and speaks in the Log-Book of a god penetrating and dominating the mind, which must fight back. The mind may combat its possessor as Jacob wrestled with his angel, but it is none the less in its power; and with that image we can move on from the prose to the poetry, where the problem is stated in full, and, since a poem must be a solution, an answer is suggested.

At first it will only be poetry in the raw state, a piece of that *Poésie Brute* which Valéry included in *Mélange*. This one is called *Chant de L'Idée-Maîtresse*, the triumph song of the idea over the mind and body to which it has come.

Viens à l'aide! Sois une chair et une charpente,
Sois ma forme, mes yeux, ma langue . . .

The idea that is singing goes on to describe its own genesis:

D'abord je n'étais pas. Ensuite, je naquis parmi tes pensées.
Je n'étais que l'une d'entre elles. Infuse, vague.
Mais maintenant tu n'es plus tout entier toi-même . . .
Je suis la seule idée qui soit conforme à ton être, et toi
L'homme qui me convient . . .
Je suis venue comme un hasard dans l'agitation de ta tête.

The mind's astonishment at its own inspiration is set out,

Ton intelligence ordinaire s'étonnera elle-même;
Elle trouvera de tels chemins que tu t'apparaîtras insensé . . .
Tu ne comprendras pas ta propre perspicacité . . .
Tu seras honteux de gagner de tels gains.
Tu murmureras humblement des merveilles.

But the reciprocity of the action is set down too, with the idea saying:

Oh! pourtant, quel miracle pour moi,
Ce mauvais corps, cet individu chétif,
Cette santé chancelante . . .
Tant d'autres hommes ne m'ont pas eue.

And at the end come these lines:

Maintenant, nous nous appartenons. On se confond,
On s'aime!
Tu es mon *Fou-à-cause-de-moi*: TON IDÉE.

From this it is only one step to *La Pythie*. We have met her already in the prose, but in the poem which bears her name she is illuminated, existing in her own right, the pythoness of Delphi in her cave, 'the motivating and sensitive monster hidden in its bony cavern', as Valéry says of the brain in *Petites Études, Mélange*. There is an echo of a serpent in her name; 'un vipère' occurs in the poem; she is described as wearing 'ornements vipérins' and sitting on a tripod which is twined round by a snake; she is 'profondément mordue'. All these are worth remembering, along with the legend that Cassandra was given her prophetic powers by being licked behind the ear by a serpent, for this knot of snakes will have to be unravelled later, when we come to the *Ébauche d'un Serpent* and *Jeune Parque*. But for the moment the names of Cassandra and the Delphic Oracle will set this pythoness in her context. We saw earlier how Valéry adopted the Nietzschean division of the mind into Apollo and Dionysus, the light and the dark. But it was not Dionysus who possessed these priestesses and seers, not the god of wine-dark lecherous intoxication. It is Apollo. It is with Apollo, 'intelligence adultère' as she says, that the pythoness must have relations, so close they can only be set down in sexual terms–possession in every sense of the word.

The darker side of the mind is here as well. In the course of the poem, almost entirely a monologue on the part of the pythoness, she speaks of 'mes ténèbres', 'l'ouragan des songes', 'épais troupeau des épouvantes', but it is not only this that is involved. 'Qui m'illumine?' she asks, but the nature of that illumination, 'épouvantable éclair', might be the lightning-flash either of idea or of dream, as might be the sparks struck from her forehead by the hands of the god–or by chance. There is indeed some kind of unification between these two minds which are after all only one mind. The pythoness cries,

> Mes deux natures vont s'unir

but it is a cry of distress, as if this union merely augments the terror.

Does Valéry mean that all thought, of whatever kind and in whatsoever manifestation, is a violence enacted on the body, a rape that nearly severs the living soul? This poem is the lament of the body at the inroads made upon it,

> Mon cher corps . . . Forme préférée,
> .   .   .   .
>
> Quelle alliance nous vécûmes,
> Avant que le don des écumes
> Ait fait de toi ce corps de mort!
>
> Mais une vierge consacrée
> Une conque neuve et nacrée
> Ne doit à la divinité
> Que sacrifice et que silence . . .

One could find prose passages which support this view, the one in *A, Mauvaises Pensées*, 'Every thought is an exception to a general rule which is not to think', or Socrates' remark in *Eupalinos* 'When you think, do you not feel that you are secretly disarranging something?'

This, however, is not the final answer of the poem. At the beginning the pythoness cries,

> Hélas! Entr'ouverte aux esprits,
> J'ai perdu mon propre mystère!

So, too, St John planted the name MYSTERY on the brows of a harlot. But at the end of the poem, the mystery and the impurity are both absolved:–

> Une attente sainte la penche,
> Car une voix nouvelle et blanche
> Échappe de ce corps impur.

The sudden introduction of whiteness, as if to efface the memory of the Scarlet Woman, is interesting and apocalyptic again, and immediately after it comes this, the final verse, which is so important I give it in full:

> *Honneur des hommes, Saint Langage,*
> *Discours prophétique et paré,*
> *Belles chaînes en qui s'engage*
> *Le dieu dans la chair égaré,*
> *Illumination, largesse!*
> *Voici parler une Sagesse*
> *Et sonner cette auguste Voix*
> *Qui se connaît quand elle sonne*
> *N'être plus la voix de personne*
> *Tant que des ondes et des bois!*

At first sight it seems almost an irrelevance; but when one looks into it, it is clearly the only answer Valéry could give– though not perhaps the only one that could be given. Words are the mind's one defence against possession by thought or dreams; even Jacob kept trying to find out the name of the angel he wrestled with. Words made into poetry, the prophetic ornamented discourse, carefully chained lest too much freedom should let in the powers of darkness–these will effect such resolution as can be achieved between the logical and the irrational functions of the mind, as Valéry says in *Mémoires d'un Poème, Variété V*. But apart from this, see how curiously this verse runs: there is the word, sanctified, a god in the flesh, the true light and glory, coming into the world–it is impossible to set it down like that and not be instantly reminded of the opening of St John's Gospel, where we started. But this time it is 'Au commencement était le Verbe', in the beginning was the Word, and it is Valéry quoting it and saying 'But the word is nothing else than one of the most precise names for that which I have called mind (*esprit*). Mind and word are almost synonymous in a great many uses. The term which is translated as "word" in the Vulgate is the Greek *logos* which also means "calculation", "reasoning", "speech", "discourse", "knowledge", as well as expression' (*La Liberté de l'Esprit, Regards sur le Monde Actuel*).

I am not parodying St John, nor, most surely, was Valéry. There is a mystery here; Valéry takes it as far as he can, and that is all we can ask of him. We are left in any case face to face with the created world linked in some way with the word, and, for Valéry, with poetry. The poet's mind and word must make his own universe, and we can go on to see how it will be done in Valéry's *Amphion*, that counterpart of the Orpheus myth where the poet subjugates all created things. The mind moves out into the world of things and people, and the pythoness leaves us at last the sea and the woods, where the *Cimetière Marin* may lie on Mediterranean slopes,

> And the branches sway and sing like the sighing strand,
> While they break out of this green world,
>   From one mirror to another.[1]

V

> '*Tree,*' *said Merlyn. At once there was*
> *an enormous mulberry growing in the middle*
> *of the courtyard . . .*
> '*They do it with mirrors,*' *said Sir Ector.*
>   T. H. WHITE

'Prose is never anything but a second-best, *mon cher*', says Mephistopheles in *Mon Faust*. So far the balance between prose and poetry in our study of Valéry has been in favour of the former; but from now on we can turn more to poetry, for the themes of Valéry's thought are becoming clearer, and it is the poems that will knit them up. *Le Cimetière Marin* is a good point at which to shift the balance. The poems dealt with so far, the Narcissus group and *La Pythie*, have lent other mouths to Valéry's thoughts, and the same thing is true of *Ébauche d'un Serpent* and *La Jeune Parque* which are still to come. *Le Cimetière Marin*, however, is not indirect but direct speech. According to the poet it was to be 'a monologue of "myself"' in which the simplest and most constant themes of my emotional and intellectual life . . . were to be invoked, interwoven, set one against another' (*Au Sujet du 'Cimetière Marin', Variété III*).

The directly personal nature of this poem makes it in some ways more difficult than the others. Figures and images are for all minds fairly common ground, whereas one mind can be foreign country for another mind. For this reason we will start,

[1] Sacheverell Sitwell.

34

not with a recapitulation of the intellectual themes in the poem, still less with a commentary or interpretation, of which there are plenty already, but with figures and images; and will call in as well one figure of the imagination, the Amphion of Valéry's poetic drama. This is a myth like that of Orpheus, the hero receiving from a god the gift of music and the power to rearrange and order creation by this means.

> Ce toit tranquille, où marchent des colombes,
> Entre les pins palpite, entre les tombes;
> Midi le juste y compose de feux
> La mer, la mer, toujours recommencée!

These first four lines of *Le Cimetière Marin* will provide what we need: trees, the sun, the sea, and a roof which implies a building and architecture. 'Orpheus with his lute made trees . . .'–that song, too, leads on to sun and sea, with the constructive power of the poet at the back of it all. We will take them in order.

Le Cimetière Marin comes from *Charmes*. In this collection two poems, *Au Platane* and *Palme*, have trees for their subject; but the odd thing is that one could almost consider the title of the collection as a tree-pun, for 'charme' in French means 'hornbeam' as well as 'charm', and this tree is mentioned in the *Platane* along with plane, pine, poplar, holm-oak, maple, aspen and beech. There are two prose poems about trees in *Poésie Brute*, *Mélange*, and another in *Autres Rhumbs*, *Tel Quel II*. The longest tree-piece is, naturally, the *Dialogue de l'Arbre* which contains prose and poetry and fables and identifications of trees with the soul, with love, with a woman. Oaks, beeches and chestnuts are specified as part of the background for *Amphion*, and as Tityre's flute figures his tree in the *Dialogue*, so Honegger's music may have formed a background for the play, one with the forest into which in the first ballet in *Amphion* the dancers disappear with the coming of night.

In a lecture given in 1931 (*Au Concert Lamoureux en 1893, Pièces sur l'Art*), Valéry compares music to a magic forest; but trees do not mean only music to him, they mean his own art, poetry, as well. Valéry loved music in his own way, envying it its scope and purity, but he loved it mainly for what it aroused in him, the workings of his own mind, as he admits in *Choses Tues*, *Tel Quel I*. In *Rhumbs*, *Tel Quel II*, he makes the interesting remark, 'Music beautiful by *transparence*, and poetry by *reflection*.' It is as if words had to silver one side of the glass in the mind and let it reflect the world of things, which music does not do. So the thing we are thinking about here, the tree, passes over from music to poetry, and in another prose poem, *À Grasse III* in *Mélange* where appear almond, olive, pine and Judas tree, Valéry says of sunrise over the trees, 'Names have definitively alighted upon things.' Words come with daylight; and so we come to our second figure, the sun.

35

The sun blazes through the whole substance of *Le Cimetière Marin*, though there is one sidelong glance at the moon,

> . . . Mais rendre la lumière
> Suppose d'ombre une morne moitié.

The sun is one of those 'three or four incontestable deities: the Sea, the Sky, the Sun', of which Valéry speaks in *Inspirations Méditerranéennes, Variété III*. It may be a god, or it may be a god's attribute, and that god is Apollo. It is he who in *Amphion* is saluted under the titles Master of the Light, Cause of the Sun, and who gives Amphion the lyre. Towards the end of the play there is a choric hymn to the Sun, conjuring him to look upon the temple built in his honour by the power of music. So sun, music and architecture come together.

And sun and sea melt into one another, a unity

> que l'Océan constelle
> D'écume qu'il arrache aux miroirs du soleil.

The sea appears constantly in Valéry's work, in numerous poems in *Album de Vers Anciens* from which the above lines are taken, in *Charmes* and *La Jeune Parque*, and scattered all through the prose. In *Le Cimetière Marin* it is linked with the same themes as were the sun and the trees. Its music is suggested, and it is the roof of the first and last lines of the poem, a wonderful image of the sea's surface as a roof of gold with a thousand tiles upon a

> temple simple à Minerve,
> Masse de calme et visible réserve.

Sun, sea, trees, music and architecture–that is the combination so far. It looks as if the poet might be creating a unity between things and the things of the mind, between body and spirit, Nature and himself. The opening of *Le Cimetière Marin* might suggest this too, with the line,

> Et quelle paix semble se concevoir!

But it is only seeming. In *Analecta, Tel Quel II*, Valéry says 'The self flees all created things. It withdraws from negation to negation. One might give the name 'Universe' to everything in which the self refuses to recognize itself.' It is interesting to see how, as the poem advances, there is a growing self-assertion, the self distinct from nature, particularly in the sixth to the eighth verses.

> Beau ciel, vrai ciel, regarde-moi qui change!

> L'âme exposée aux torches du solstice,
> Je te soutiens, admirable justice
>
> O pour moi seul, à moi seul, en moi-même.

In verse 13 Valéry speaks of the great sky as a mind, but his own mind is a separate entity:

> Je suis en toi le secret changement.
>
> Mes repentirs, mes doutes, mes contraintes
> Sont le défaut de ton grand diamant.

It is as if he were trying to relate everything back to his own mind. Towards the end of the poem, after the verses dealing with the dead and the living, there comes the famous verse on the Eleatic Zeno, a jump straight into abstraction, i.e. into Valéry's mind, 'a jump which breaks up and dissipates a state of sombre fixity, complementary, as it were, to the reigning splendour' (*Au Sujet du 'Cimetière Marin'*, *Variété III*). In *La Crise de l'Esprit*, *Variété*, he says that the things of the world interest him only in connection with the intellect, and in *Moralités* in *Tel Quel I* he suggests that the universe has need of a human intellect if it is to exist at all. 'Man thinks, therefore I exist', says the Universe.

Gradually everything at this stage merges into the mind, and sun, sea and trees, the background of *Le Cimetière Marin*, go the same way explicitly, for in *Rhumbs*, *Tel Quel II*, we read, 'But the sea, the trees, the suns, the human eye above all–all that is artifice.' It is the construction in the mind that matters. The world is to be reconstructed, and we are back to architecture again.

In *La Soirée avec Monsieur Teste* it is suggested that the angles of Teste's skull bore some sort of kindred relation to those of the capitals of the columns. He might be growing into a pillar–and one is reminded of the *Cantique des Colonnes* (music and architecture combined in verse) which occurs in *Charmes* and is inserted in *Amphion* as the song of the Muses, accompanying Amphion's construction of a marvellous architecture by the power of Apollonian music. The connection between music and architecture was one of Valéry's favourite themes. It is dealt with at length in *Eupalinos* and in the *Histoire d'Amphion* in *Pièces sur l'Art*, but its finest expression is in the *Cantique* itself:–

> Douces colonnes, ô
> L'orchestre de fuseaux!
>
> Nous chantons à la fois
> Que nous portons les cieux!

Vois quels hymnes candides
Quelle sonorité
Nos éléments limpides
Tirent de la clarté!

That might seem the last word, Olympian control and beauty in the world of things made perfect by the operations of music and architecture in the constructive mind. But it is not. There is an undertone to this classical harmony, a different and deep-sea current, a spot in the sun, an image in the mirror. It runs all through *Le Cimetière Marin* if you look for it, coming out at the very end into the open. It does not matter which path you take–sun, sea, trees, music, architecture, the three poems we have been talking about–they all come to the same thing. They may all be artifice and construction, but as Eupalinos the architect says, 'By dint of all this construction, I really feel that I have ended up by constructing myself.'

If we start with architecture, we find a hint in a stage direction in *Amphion*, 'A little edifice composed of dancers [*danseuses* in the femine gender] clad in tunics assembles and takes its stand on a buttress of rock.' There follows immediately the singing of the *Cantique des Colonnes* by the Muses, who are architecture literally embodied. Eupalinos has the same thing to say, 'This delicate temple is, though no-one knows it, the mathematical image of a girl of Corinth with whom I was happy in love'; he adds later, 'When I compose a dwelling-place, be it for gods or men, . . . it seems to me that my body plays its part in it.' If we pick up the theme of music we find the same thing. Teste compares music to bodily pain, and says in *Quelques Pensées* that if we could study music and pain in this way, as similar languages, we might learn something about 'notre corps profond', the deeps of the body.

These were the two fields of mental construction with which we have been concerned. The sun, however, and the sea and the trees are equally direct ways to the same end. Starting with the sun, we find in *D, Mauvaises Pensées*, the little phrase 'Le Jour et le Corps, deux grandes puissances', as if the hours of sunlight and the body had some powerful connection. The poem *Aurore* in *Charmes* is conceived in terms of bodily similitudes. In *Poésie Brute, Mélange*, there is the following poem *To The Sun*:

Au soleil sur mon lit après l'eau
Au soleil et au reflet énorme du soleil sur la mer,
Sous ma fenêtre
Et aux reflets et aux reflets des reflets
Du soleil et des soleils sur la mer
Dans les glaces,
Après le bain, le café, les idées,

> Nu, au soleil sur mon lit tout illuminé
> > Nu, seul, fou,
> > Moi!

This joins up immediately with *Le Cimetière Marin*, the first bodily reference occurring in verse five; by verse six the body is already definite enough to cast a shadow. One is reminded of Shakespeare's

> Shine out, fair sun, till I have bought a glass,
> That I may see my shadow as I pass,

and by verse seven the body has already become the mirror of the sun, the mirror of the god, as the phrase runs in *L, Mauvaises Pensées*. So at the end of the poem it is the *body*, not the mind, which breaks out of the web of thought:

> Brisez, mon corps, cette forme pensive!
> Courons à l'onde en rejaillir vivant!

But the sea he runs to and the trees he runs from tell the same story, though adding one thing more which we saw in a glass darkly in the last two chapters. It is in this way that Valéry describes the sea ('sea' in French is feminine) and the swimmer, 'Here the whole body gives itself . . . He manipulates *her*, he desires to seize *her*, to embrace *her* . . . he loves and possesses *her*, and engenders with *her* a thousand strange ideas. By her I am the man I wish to be . . . *I understand to the extreme what love could be*' (*Autres Rhumbs, Tel Quel II*; the italics are Valéry's).

At the end of *Amphion*, when the hero is about to enter the temple he has built, the veiled form of a woman bars his path, a 'figure who is Love or Death,' so the stage directions say. In the earlier musings in *Le Cimetière Marin* the same thoughts had come, in verse 16,

> Le sang qui brille aux lèvres qui se rendent,
> Les derniers dons, les doigts qui les défendent,
> Tout va sous terre et rentre dans le jeu!

These girls are dead, laid among the tree roots; but the trees themselves take up the tale. In the *Dialogue de l'Arbre* Tityre says, 'I love you, great Tree, I am mad with love of your limbs . . . You know well, my Tree, that with the dawn I come to embrace you.' Later this same shepherd sings to the Great Tree of Love.

Amour–that word is caught up in the final verses of *Le Cimetière Marin*,

> Amour, peut-être, ou de moi-même haine?

The question stands between these two statements:

> Le vrai rongeur, le ver irréfutable
> N'est point pour vous qui dormez sous la table,
> Il vit de vie, il ne me quitte pas!

> Amour, peut-être, ou de moi-même haine?
> Sa dent secrète est de moi si prochaine
> Que tous les noms lui peuvent convenir!

Here is the hint of the serpent who appears in *La Jeune Parque*; but so far it is only a shadow of one, *Ébauche d'un Serpent*, and to that we turn next. For there is an older story here; 'The most astonishing tree-story is that of the giant apple-trees of which the fruit of one offered to the eater of its fabulous flesh a life eternal, while that of the other produced at the first taste a strange clarity in the mind of the eater: he was invaded by a shame attached to the things of love . . . and felt his nakedness to be a crime and a branding' *(Le Dialogue de l'Arbre)*. No mind without a body, Narcissus said; no sun without a moon, the pythoness said; here everything says: no Adam without Eve. It is the final, and most difficult case of two becoming one. At the end of *Le Cimetière Marin* we are left with trees, love, serpent and woman –and we are running to Paradise.

VI

> Basilisk: *fabulous serpent whose gaze,*
> *it was said, had the power to kill . . .*
> *It was believed that the basilisk killed*
> *itself if it looked at itself in a mirror.*
> LAROUSSE DU XXe SIÈCLE

'In the relationship between man and woman all is magic.' That saying of Valéry's, in *G, Mauvaises Pensées*, reminds one of the Book of Proverbs, where the writer says, 'There be three things which are too wonderful for me, yea, four which I know not: The way of an eagle in the air; the way of a serpent upon a rock; the way of a ship in the midst of the sea; and the way of a man with a maid.' Valéry here mentions the last, but we shall find the others, with their particular sort of magic, in what we now come to, the poem *Ébauche d'un Serpent*, the poetic drama *Sémiramis*, which can serve as commentary on the poem as *Amphion* did last time, and, eventually, *La Jeune Parque*.

Ébauche d'un Serpent belongs, as did *Le Cimetière Marin*, to the collection to which Valéry gave the title and sub-title: '*Charmes* (c'est à dire: *Poèmes*).' In *Mémoires d'un Poème, Variété V*, he says

40

that the object of poetry is the creation of a state of enchantment. In this poem the poetry itself is to work the magic and create the world in which all lovers move. It is not entirely new ground, however, for in *Le Cimetière Marin* the charm had already begun. All four of the Proverbial mysteries, the ways of birds and ships, the ways of serpents and of lovers, are in that poem, and the magic is beginning to draw them together. The first and last lines fuse doves and ships (the image being that of the sea as a roof on which peck the dipping sails); and strangely enough the other two are fused as well, as we saw, the worm that dieth not, being called in the next breath 'Amour peut-être.' We must gather this up now and go on to see how the magic works in *Ébauche d'un Serpent*. This is more dangerous ground, for the snake is there now explicit. 'Surely the serpent will bite without enchantment', as Ecclesiastes says, and Valéry here seems almost to be trying, by his *Charmes*, which are poems, to hold off the serpent's tooth.

The nature of the magic and of the world it will make can be guessed from another passage, called *Magic*, in *L, Mauvaises Pensées*. 'At this moment the cock crew and did not crow, and it was not a cock–and perhaps there was–no moment. The wind freshened and did not freshen–and the sky, white all over with stars, had never existed.' It might be dawn over Eden itself. With its birds which are not birds and stars which are not stars, this is an anti-Aristotelian world, which no longer obeys the demand of logic that something shall not be at one and the same time itself and its opposite. Here everything can be its own self and its own contradiction, simultaneously.

This type of magic holds good all through the *Ébauche* and *Sémiramis*. In the latter, our own particular star, the sun, becomes a bird in Act III ('Day dawns . . . the Eagle comes'); a woman also becomes a bird, for at the end of the play Sémiramis is changed into a dove. Valéry suggests elsewhere, in *Psaume Z, Mélange*, that a woman may become a snake; one remembers *Lamia* and the Lady Geraldine of *Christabel*; but there is an older tale than these which belongs where we belong in this chapter, in Eden itself, the legend of Lilith, Adam's first wife who was at once woman, snake and devil. We can work round in circles here, however–a well-attested technique in magic–for a serpent can be a bird, 'reptile aux extases d'oiseau' as Valéry's serpent says in the *Ébauche*, and one remembers the serpents and doves who appear side by side in the Gospels (St Matthew, X, 16) and the scene in *Alice in Wonderland*:

'I'm–I'm a little girl,' said Alice, rather doubtfully, as she remembered the number of changes she had gone through that day.

'A likely story indeed!' said the Pigeon in a tone of the

41

deepest contempt . . . 'You're a serpent; and there's no use denying it.'

That happened in Wonderland woods; but this is Eden where the snake is that old serpent Lucifer, who was also the morning star, and who is the subject of Valéry's poem. The mention of Alice is helpful, however, if only to remind us of something we should have realized all along: that if we chose a mirror for image we should come to the stage where things are in reverse, as the writing of Jabberwocky was reversed before Alice's eyes, and as prayers run backwards in black magic.

In *Ébauche d'un Serpent*, verse eight, the serpent speaks of itself as a 'sombre miroir'. St Thomas Aquinas says of an angel that 'he is a pure and most clear mirror'[1], and a fallen angel may retain the mirror of the mind, even though it be a black one. 'I was an Archangel', says the Devil in Valéry's *Mon Faust*, Act I, Scene I, and Valéry draws his own distinction between angel and devil in *Autres Rhumbs*, *Tel Quel II*: 'The Angel differs from the demon only by one certain reflection which has not so far presented itself to him.' Valéry knew St Thomas (there is a direct reference to him in *Cahier B* 1910, *Tel Quel I*), and says, a little mockingly, in the Preface to *Monsieur Teste* that theology tends to turn up everywhere. He held no beliefs, and the religious themes which occur so often in his work are tantalizing because one cannot help wondering how far they are deliberate. *Sémiramis* provides an interesting example in Act III; the four idols in the stage setting are described as follows: 'Sed, *bull with a human face*; Nergal, *lion with a human face*; Oustour, *man*; Nattig, *headed like an eagle*.' When one looks at these, they turn out to be the symbols of the four Evangelists. It is impossible to say whether this is intentional, and still more impossible when we come to the serpent of the *Ébauche*. After all, it befits the subtle, double-tongued serpent who speaks the poem to be ambiguous. It is best hunted as men hunted the basilisk, with a mirror.

The poem opens in the garden, as if all were primal simplicity –the foliage, the moving airs, the green triangle of the snake's head, the smile pierced by a tooth. Trees and sun are here again, as they were in the last poem, but they are not merely trees and sun any more, for by the magic they become converted or *translated* according to the phrase in the *Midsummer Night's Dream*. The image in the mirror is subject to reversal.

The sun is the first to undergo such a translation. The serpent addresses it as 'O roi des ombres fait de flamme', as if its essence were darkness and not light. Valéry quotes with admiration in *Littérature*, *Tel Quel I*, the line by Victor Hugo: 'Un affreux soleil noir d'où rayonne la nuit.' The ambiguity, or the light that is

[1] *Summa Theologica*, Part I, Q. 58, Art. 4.

darkness, deepens as the poem progresses. There is some sort of affinity between sun and serpent, the latter addressing the former as 'Toi, le plus fier de mes complices,' the proudest of my accomplices. With verse six, however, God comes into the picture as well.

> Celui qui règne dans les cieux
> D'une voix qui fut la lumière
> Ouvrit l'univers spacieux.

Yet Lucifer also was a star, the first and greatest of them all, according to the Devil in *Mon Faust* ('I may have fallen, but from the greatest height'), and according to the poem too:

> Mais, le premier mot de son Verbe,
> Moi!... Des astres le plus superbe
> Qu'ait parlés le fou créateur,
> Je suis!

There is another ambiguity here, for the MOI might refer to Satan, but it might almost refer back to the *Verbe* as well, and the whole passage is strangely reminiscent of the name God gave Himself: I AM WHO AM. Under the heading of *Le Moi* in *Suite, Tel Quel II*, Valéry says, 'It is in the Scriptures that one finds the cult of the self expressed in its most ingenuous, brutal, absolute form. But it is the self of God.'

Already God and Devil seem to have become in some way ambivalent. In the very next verse we see them face to face in the mirror.

> Objet radieux de ma haine...
> Regardez-vous dans ma ténèbre!
> Devant votre image funèbre,
> Orgueil de mon sombre miroir,
> Si profond fut votre malaise
> Que votre souffle sur la glaise
> Fut un soupir de désespoir!

It is a counterpart of the scene at the end of *Sémiramis* where the queen says to the sun, 'Hail, Lord of Time... I desire only You for my mirror... and in all Sémiramis there shall be no secrets nor darkness for you.' She, the self-avowed embodiment of pride, lifted up on her tower into union with the sun, matches the serpent whose sin was also 'Pride that struck down the morning star from heaven', and who is lifted up to heaven on a tall tree.

Even the tree, however, with which the poem opens and closes, is subtle as well as simple. The last five verses of the poem are a hymn to the tree, balancing the hymn to the sun in the first half,

> Arbre, grand Arbre, Ombre des Cieux,
> Irrésistible Arbre des arbres.

But the tree figures infinity by lifting its head into the sun and sending its roots down to the dark places of the earth, and one remembers in the *Dialogue de l'Arbre* the story of the primeval tree which grew till it covered all Asia; 'Uplifting its intense solitude into the clean-cut blue, it was the God Tree.' Here, too, it is a shadow of Heaven and harbours a 'colombe prédestinée', predestined dove. But it harbours a snake as well, and again one is struck by a double potentiality in the lines referring to one who 'Sur ton branchage vient se tordre.' It might be the serpent or God who is twisted on the branches of a tree, just as Moses' serpent twisted on a rod was an antitype of the Crucifixion (St John, III, 14).

So at the beginning there is a sun and at the end a tree, and each figures in some way both God and devil, who in turn figure one another. Between sun and tree stands Eve, but not in separation, for the sun and the tree seem to be united with her, almost physically. The serpent speaks of

> Son flanc vaste et d'or parcouru
> Ne craignant le soleil ni l'homme

as if sun and man were interchangeable; in the same way Sémiramis finally consummates what might almost be called a marriage with the sun. The tree too has bodily affinities with Eve. It responds physically to her touch when she reaches out to pluck the apple:

> Tout l'Arbre de la Connaissance . . .
> Agitait son grand corps . . .

and, earlier, occurs this:

> Mais quel souffle sous le sein sombre
> Que mordait l'Arbre de son ombre!

as if the tree were tempted humanity and Eve's breast the apple.

The emphasis the whole time is upon unity. It is worth remembering that the serpent is still at this stage describing humanity before the Fall, when, as theology teaches, man was in union and at peace with God, creation and himself. The Genesis narrative shows how each of these unities was broken. With Valéry, however, we are looking at the scene in the mirror, and in this poem it is not God who is the source of unity. On the contrary, the serpent outdoes God in its passion for unity and perfection, and it is this that is communicated to Eve and her kindred.

44

The serpent's conviction that

> l'univers n'est qu'un défaut
> Dans la pureté du Non-être!

has been much quoted, but it is only a stage in the argument. It is the exact opposite of St Thomas, who says, 'God is Being itself, Subsistent, absolutely undetermined' (*Summa Theologica*, Part I, Q. 11, Art. 4). For the serpent, however, Not-Being is the perfection, and the creation was an initial fall on the part of the Creator. In *Autres Rhumbs, Tel Quel II*, Valéry talks of the fall of the angels and that of man, and goes on 'But a Creation is the first of these breaches.' The theme is developed in the poem:

> Comme las de son pur spectacle,
> Dieu lui-même a rompu l'obstacle
> De sa parfaite éternité;
> Il se fit Celui qui dissipe
> En conséquences, son Principe,
> En étoiles, son Unité.

The serpent sees creation as imperfection, and hates it, and God, on that account,

> je hais le Nom qui crée
> Tant de prodiges imparfaits!

But the hatred springs from the love it had for perfection and hence for God whom it had loved out of all measure–'Vous que j'aimais éperdument.' Thus God's image looks out of this dark mirror.

Describing itself, the serpent says, 'Je suis Celui qui modifie'; but if we are right, the modification will not be towards greater imperfection, since that is what the serpent abhors. It will be an attempt to communicate to man the satanic passion for perfection and unity.

One thing is clear in the poem: the temptation is not directed to the mind. Neither is it directed to Adam, of whom there is no mention. In *Suite, Tel Quel II*, Valéry invents a small sub-myth of his own in which the brain is Adam and the nervous or sympathetic system is Eve: 'the brain, straightforward, not very profound, naked ... chained to this serpent or woman of the nerves who knows more about things and less about things than he does.' The rational mind is bound to be nearer to clarity and unity than this other strange system to which it is wedded, the sentient body, the seat of the heart and, Valéry would add, the soul. He discusses the Christian doctrine of the Incarnation in those very terms in *Cahier B 1910, Tel Quel I*. The serpent too, though it may be 'esprit' and 'intelligence', is a body as well

45

–'Bête je suis, mais bête aiguë'–and is in its own way a reverse image of the Incarnation, as Valéry hints in *Psaume Z, Mélange*.

It is to this obscure half of the human being that the serpent addresses itself. Eve, the first woman, naked and beautiful, appears all through the poem little more than a body, and it is to the body or the heart or the soul that the overtures are made.

> Je retouche au cœur qui s'y fie,
> D'un doigt sûr et mystérieux!
>
> Je disparais dans un cœur pur!
> Fut-il jamais de sein si dur
> Qu'on n'y puisse loger un songe?

The final temptation runs in this fashion:

> Âme, disais-je, doux séjour
> De toute extase prohibée,
> Sens-tu la sinueuse amour
> Que j'ai du Père dérobée?
>
> Du plaisir que tu te proposes
> Cède, cher corps, cède aux appâts!...
> Danse, cher corps... Ne pense pas!

It only hints its meaning, but the hint is enough:

> Ce lieu charmant qui vit la chair
> Choir et se joindre m'est très cher!

It is as if the Fall meant the fall of Adam and Eve into an access of passion ('And the eyes of them both were opened, and they knew that they were naked') and into one another's arms.

It seems a simple temptation to animality; but it is not simple, just as the 'animale simplicité' of the serpent is a device, the serpent says, 'qui me déguise'. It is not just the bodily labyrinth of sensibility and passion which is the trap, any more than it is the mind. It is the *Eritis sicut Dei*, the Biblical tempter's words on which Valéry twice comments. In *Amor VI, Mélange*, we find it said that there is one thing which makes us like the gods 'or perhaps superior to them': the union of love and the mind. This too is a turning towards unity and perfection. The intellect might attain to unity on its own. This is what lies at the back of the second part of *Mon Faust* where Le Solitaire invokes the perfection of intellectual purity

> contre mon corps, contre mon âme,
> Contre le temps, contre le sexe et le sommeil,

Contre la vie et le désir et le regret . . .
Contre ce qui connaît et ce qui sent;
Contre moi-même, que je hais comme une épouse.

The mind alone might be able to reach some such state of complete, isolated, lunatic purity, but Le Solitaire is a myth even for Valéry. Teste himself is married, and the remarkable letter of Madame Émile Teste tells us something of the ménage. The mind cannot separate itself from soul and body and passion and the heart; and the heart is love, and love requires an object.

In that fact is hidden the serpent's tooth, for love desires perfect union with the beloved, and is thereby betrayed, for, humanly speaking, such union is not possible, though the desire for it is god-like and therefore capable of being turned to diabolical ends. *Psaume Z* in *Mélange* says so clearly:

Ma satisfaction est un fantôme; jamais tu ne pourras l'atteindre.
N'est-ce point l'*Éternel* qui a créé son offenseur?
Ne l'a-t-il point tiré de sa préscience volontaire?
Ne l'a-t-il pas appelé dans un jardin?
N'a-t-il point pris une chair pour le mieux connaître? . . .
Ils ont été aux profondes parties de la nuit . . .
Ils ont noué le jour qui cesse aux jour qui naît, par les nœuds de leurs membres.
Ils ont connu leur unité; ils ont croisé leurs forces; ils se sont respirés l'un l'autre longuement.
Toutes fois ils s'ignoreront toujours.

Lovers are no more one than the parallel mirrors to which Valéry compares them in *Au Sujet d'"Adonis", Variété*.

It is not only that man is betrayed by woman, though Valéry suggests this, as the story of the Fall does also, and has bitter things to say of her. 'Woman is the enemy of the mind, whether she gives love or refuses it' (*E, Mauvaises Pensées*); 'God created man, and finding that he was not lonely enough, gave him a woman for companion to make him realize his loneliness all the more' (*Moralités, Tel Quel I*). This is not the voice of contempt and resentment, however; it is the voice of pain, at the inability to fuse this separateness into full and perfect union which the soul craves and cannot achieve. The serpent in the *Ébauche* achieves its purpose and communicates to mortals its own mock-divine thirst for perfection:–

Il me suffit que dans les airs,
L'immense espoir des fruits amers
Affole les fils de la fange

but in the end its triumph is despair,

> Offrant à la gloire de Dieu
> Le triomphe de ma tristesse,

just as, earlier, God's breath upon the dust of the ground which was to be man was 'un soupir de désespoir'.

'Love consists in the feeling that one has handed over to another, in spite of oneself, that which was for oneself alone' (*Choses Tues, Tel Quel I*). With this comes a terrifying intensification of the mirror-image, for Narcissus speaks in just such terms, rejecting the love of women, the outward turning, and adoring himself as the nearest approach to perfection, perfect loneliness offered up almost as a religious sacrifice, as Sémiramis ('O véritable Moi, Seule Sémiramis . . . ô force d'être unique'), is offered up on the altar of the Sun. She too had attempted the fusion of one self with another, in love, as the song in Act II tells:

> Au cœur de la Nuit,
> Cher Toi qui es Moi . . .
> Nous sommes un seul
> Au cœur de la Nuit.

The union ends with the murder of her lover by the queen, and in Act III there is a total renunciation of love, and a passionate turning to the self, until at the last the self has exalted itself to the level of God:

> je ne serai plus par l'amour
> Pareille à toutes les femmes . . .
> O Dieu des Dieux, il n'y a que Vous et que Moi . . .
> Je le veux de toutes mes forces.

This is the cult of the self as an inversion of love too pure and intense to be satisfied, the voice of the serpent,

> Cette inimitable saveur
> Que tu ne trouves qu'à toi-même!

But the cult is self-annihilating, for if perfection lies only in the self, and Non-Being is better than Being, the conclusion is obvious. Narcissus vanishes, Sémiramis disappears in a burst of sunlight, and one begins to understand why suicide is so often discussed in Valéry's work (in *L'Idée Fixe, Tel Quel I* and *II*, and in an article *Sur le Suicide* which appeared in the *Révolution Surréaliste* in January, 1925). There is a possible explanation, too, of those sudden cries of pain which come so strangely now and again: 'Angoisse, mon véritable métier'—anguish, my real vocation. If Teste is of glass, he has undone himself, for he is as it were the mirror between God and devil, and unable to commit himself either way: 'Man cannot, in sincerity, either sell himself to the devil or give himself to God' (*Choses Tues, Tel Quel I*).

The only other answer seems to be to break the mirror; but instead we find Valéry questioning it once more. The remarkable passage which opens *Cahier B* 1910 runs as follows:

> Late tonight there shines in greater simplicity this reflection of my nature: instinctive horror and detachment from the particularity of human life . . . Loves, joys, agonies, all feelings terrify or bore me . . . chained to that which suffers, hopes, implores, flagellates itself, alongside my fragment of purity.

Then comes the strange question, addressed to that ambiguous image in the mirror, 'Why do you devour me when I had foreseen your tooth?' Valéry suggested as the device of the martyr, 'I prefer to die rather than to reflect' (*Rhumbs, Tel Quel II*), but his own might be the looking-glass version of this; sooner reflect than die. The answer is not suicide. It is somewhere in that complete reflection of Valéry, *La Jeune Parque*, and we have to try to find it.

VII

> *. . . the water becommeth Cristal &*
> *upon that groweth the good diamondes.*
> SIR JOHN MANDEVILLE

To make any work of art is to make—or rather to unmake and remake—oneself. 'There is only one thing to do: to remake oneself' (*P, Mauvaises Pensées*); and as Valéry adds, 'It is not a simple matter.' *La Jeune Parque* was for Valéry a protracted poetic exercise. He talks in various places of its conception and composition, particularly in *Fragments des Mémoires d'un Poème* and *Le Prince et la Jeune Parque* in *Variété V*, and in *Souvenir* in *Mélange*. In the first and second of these he gives some idea of his literary aims in the poem, comparing them with the effect of modulation in music and of recitative. In the third, he suggests that he started with form, and allowed the 'content' of his thought (the quotation marks are his) to be determined by the form. This is not perversity or error; it is the right way round, for if the poem is to be not merely an excretion of words but a reconstruction of the self, this can only be achieved through form. The content of the self is given; one can only re-form. This is not figurative speech. To make a poem is to remake oneself, and Valéry says so in connection with this poem, 'I made for myself a form of poetry

49

. . . which had no other aim, and practically no other law, than to set up for me a way of living with myself' (*Souvenir, Mélange*). He had written no poetry for twenty years, and his return to it was not merely a return to an old and half-forgotten practice but also to 'a region of the mind which I had abandoned and even fled from.'

Such a making and remaking is, inevitably, an ordeal, and as is the habit of minds which have some great thing to face, Valéry goes to the setting which he loves most dearly as if to draw strength from it, the seashore in the very early morning, with the stars still visible and the wind cold but with the promise of dawn in the air, the time of day in which Valéry did much of his thinking and to which in his prose and poetry he constantly turns, as if for momentary refreshment.

It is in this setting that *La Jeune Parque* opens, with a sense of foreboding,

> Qui pleure là, sinon le vent simple, à cette heure
> Seule avec diamants extrêmes? . . . Mais qui pleure,
> Si proche de moi-même au moment de pleurer?

but with the stars and the sea in communion with the self,

> La houle me murmure une ombre de reproche

> Je scintille, liée à ce ciel inconnu.

This self is disguised, or figured, in the person of La Jeune Parque who speaks the poem. The title has been thought obscure, as Valéry says in the mocking little commentary in verse which he wrote on the poem, *Le Philosophe et 'La Jeune Parque'*:–

> Chaque mortel qui n'a point cure
> De songer ni d'approfondir,
> Au seul nom que je porte a tôt fait de bondir.

One can come to it, however, by stages. After what we saw in the last chapter, we might expect the speaker to be a woman, the feminine principle in any personality, for, as Valéry says in *Instants, Mélange*, every man contains a hidden woman. In the end, however, it comes to the same thing, for Monsieur and Madame Teste are married and one, and Valéry denounces the coarse distinction between sensibility and intelligence (*Mémoires d'un Poème, Variété V*). The best way of expressing this in the poem was clearly a myth, that being a form of thought in which the content is immaterial but into which any mind can think itself. Valéry demands of thought that in its presentation it should be as clear and impersonal as a phenomenon from another world (ibid.). All of this fits La Jeune Parque, the Young Fate; but she by her name and quality adds one thing more, the notion of life and death over which the Fates preside; as we have seen, this was no mean question in Valéry's mind, and the poem vacillates between life and death.

> Rien ne me murmurait qu'un désir de mourir
> Dans cette blonde pulpe au soleil pût mûrir.

She comes to us with a question which has been foreshadowed already:

> J'interroge mon cœur quelle douleur l'éveille,
> Quel crime par moi-même ou sur moi consommé?

And with her come multiple reflections, concentrated in herself, of all the other themes and forms which we have met in Valéry. The serpent is here:

> J'y suivais un serpent qui venait de me mordre

winding in and out of the poem, mentioned in the epigraph at the beginning and in practically every section until the last. Teste is here:

> Je me voyais me voir . . .

> Je garde loin de vous, l'esprit sinistre et clair.

Here is Narcisse:

> . . . une vierge à soi-même enlacée,
> Jalouse . . .

> . . . la chair vide baise une sombre fontaine.

Here is the Pythoness:

> L'esprit n'est pas si pur que jamais idolâtre
> Sa fougue solitaire aux élans de flambeau
> Ne fasse fuir les murs de son morne tombeau.

> Je pense, sur le bord doré de l'univers,
> A ce goût de périr qui prend la Pythonisse
> En qui mugit l'espoir que le monde finisse.

Here are Sémiramis and the *Cantique des Colonnes*:

> J'étais l'égale et l'épouse du jour,
> Seul support souriant que je formais d'amour
> À la toute-puissante altitude adorée.

Here, united as in *Eupalinos*, are a temple and a body:

> 'Que dans le ciel placés, mes yeux tracent mon temple!
> Et que sur moi repose un autel sans exemple!'
> Criaient de tout mon corps la pierre et la pâleur.

Here are the shadow on the ground in the sun and the *blonde argile* of *Le Cimetière Marin*:

> Vers mes sens lumineux nageait ma blonde argile . . .
> Si ce n'est, ô Splendeur, qu'à mes pieds l'Ennemie,
> Mon ombre! . . .

There is no space to mention it all in detail–the adoration of the body, the rejection of dreams, the horror of life mingled with compassion–'J'ai pitié de nous tous, ô tourbillons de poudre!'–just as Valéry had, in *Choses Tues*, *Tel Quel I*, appropriated to himself God's words, *Misereor super turbam*, the light and darkness of the self, the sun-god, trees, dancers, the sea, and, finally, the three mirrors of the poem.

Each in turn is lighted up, only to be reflected back again into and in favour of the self, 'Harmonieuse Moi', 'Mystérieuse Moi', which draws all these reflections together. The mirror image seems to have come back, but with a difference. With all these reflections at once it may seem to have become bewilderingly complicated, like the poem itself. The bewilderment, however, is only the result of our having not yet transformed ourselves to the image, or transformed the image itself. It is concentration we are faced with, the concentration in one person, Jeune Parque, Valéry, oneself, of all these possible existences. 'In every man, given the same materials of flesh and mind, several "personalities" are possible, coexisting sometimes, more or less in equality' (*Analecta*, *Tel Quel II*).

In the last two chapters we have watched these potential existences drawing closer and closer together, until in *La Jeune Parque* they are united. They cannot all be recapitulated here; only reading and re-reading of the poem can call them up. Only the poem, too, can speak its answer, the resolution and admission of all these opposed surfaces of reflection, none rejected or blackened out but each admitted as part of the complex system of refraction which lights up the work. It is a wonderful answer: the self's assent to its being, and forgiveness of itself,

Doucement,
Me voici: mon front touche à ce consentement . . .
Ce corps, je lui pardonne, et je goûte à la cendre.

the willing descent into sleep, like a sacrifice to the serpents, while the mouth consents to the loss of controlled speech and babbles profound nonsense:

Je me remets entière au bonheur de descendre,
Ouverte aux noirs témoins, les bras suppliciés,
Entre des mots sans fin, sans moi, balbutiés . . .
Abandonne-toi vive aux serpents, aux trésors.
Dors toujours! Descends, dors toujours! Descends, dors, dors.

(La porte basse c'est une bague . . . où la gaze
Passe . . . Tout meurt, tout rit dans la gorge qui jase . . .
L'oiseau boit sur ta bouche et tu ne peut le voir . . .
Viens plus bas, parle bas . . . Le noir n'est pas si noir . . .)

There is the great salute to the world in the dawn, seen as a woman's body with its rosy islands and bays; and at the last, the assent to life and to the heart, the body in its essential purity caught in the sunlight and warmed into life and, astonishingly and movingly, into gratitude.

Alors, malgré moi-même, il le faut, ô Soleil,
Que j'adore mon cœur où tu te viens connaître,
Doux et puissant retour du délice de naître,
Feu vers qui se soulève une vierge de sang
Sous les espèces d'or d'un sein reconnaissant!

How has it been done? The answer is in the form; both poem and self are in the form, and something has happened to each of them. Each of the figures here concentrated was called 'a *facet* of one system amongst those of which I am capable' (*Mémoires d'un Poème, Variété V*). Elsewhere Valéry compares sensibility to the spectrum (*Suite, Tel Quel II*). We seem to have concentrated our reflecting surfaces into one quintessential and prismatic drop, and our own minds with it–'All the poverty of life in a crystal', as Valéry says in *Poésie Brute, Mélange*.

La Jeune Parque gives the answer from the very beginning, 'Seule avec diamants extrêmes.' In the *Mémoires d'un Poème* Valéry speaks of poetry as 'a hint of diamond coming through a lump of blue clay.' In *La Jeune Parque* the stars are diamonds, just as the world is diamond-studded when seen through tears such as the Young Fate sheds: 'Vos yeux en pleurs lui voient des diamants' (*Le Philosophe et 'La Jeune Parque'*). 'Le futur lui-même Ne fut qu'un diamant' . . . 'Le gel cède à regret ses derniers diamants'–this poem is full of them, and so are the other poems. The universe is full of them; even the sea is 'solid and crystalline', 'a mass of facets' (*Autres Rhumbs, Tel Quel II*), or breaking over the Jeune Parque at the end of the poem in 'un éblouissement d'étincelles glacées', a dazzle of frozen sparks. More, the universe *is* a diamond in *Le Cimetière Marin*, with the mind inside it.

What is true of the poetry is true of the self as well. The final image is not the haunted face reflected in the looking-glass. It is the self concentrated inside the diamond of its universe and its mind, a concentration of ice and fire, and in the middle, the play of light and reflection and beyond that–nothing. '*Je m'appelle*: Personne' (*G, Mauvaises Pensées*). This is what Valéry says of a diamond in *Mélange*: 'Its beauty, so they tell me, is the result of the smallness of the angle of total reflexion. The diamond cutter arranges the facets in such a way that the ray of light which penetrates the jewel by one of them can come out only by the same one–hence the fire and brilliance. A lovely image of how I think of poetry: return of the mind's ray of light to the words by which it entered.'

But we have ourselves returned to the words by which we entered, for there is no separating one mind from another, and if this is an image of Valéry's mind, it is an image of others as well. 'The man of genius is the man who makes me a genius', Valéry says (*P, Mauvaises Pensées*). If, however, this diamond mind seems a great loneliness and a splendour utterly unlike our own, we can return to the words which headed this chapter, which are a foolishness and therefore the more suitable. None the less they say something Valéry knew: that thought, even though diamond-like and crystalline, is not left lonely to blaze in sterile impotence. 'Thought has the two sexes; cross-fertilizes itself and carries its own children.' That is Valéry, in *Littérature, Tel Quel I*; but we will end our book with an older and more childish picture: 'Good dyamondes . . . grow both togither, male and female, and are noryshed with the dewe of heaven, and they engendre commonly & bring forth small children that multiply & growe all the yeare.'

ENGLISH TRANSLATIONS OF PASSAGES
QUOTED IN THE TEXT

p. 6. A mirror rises from the sea.

p. 7. Of which mortal eyes in their full splendour are only mirrors, darkened and plaintive.

p. 23. O obedient form set opposite my eyes.

p. 23. I am alone! . . .
Alone! but none the less he who approaches himself.

p. 23. No nymph, no beloved attracts me
As thou dost upon the water, inexhaustible Myself!

p. 23. To see, o marvel, to see! my shaded mouth
Betray . . . paint upon the water a flower of thought,
And what happenings sparkle in the eye!

p. 23. O my sovereign good, beloved body, thou art all I have!

p. 23. O my body, beloved body, temple separating me
From my divinity.

p. 23. Dear treasure of a mirror which shares out the world!

p. 24. The soul, the soul with the dark eyes, reaches to night itself,
She grows immense and encounters nothing . . .
Between death and herself, what a glance is hers!

p. 26. Pale, bitten deep.

p. 26. Dead, wandering, a moon for ever.

p. 28. The excess of my tenderness belongs in darkness.

p. 29. My lucid Fountain, they have only a cloudy river
As a shadowy witness of their omnipotence.

p. 31. Come to my help! Be a flesh and framework for me, be my form, my eyes, my tongue.

p. 31. At first I was not. Then I was born among your thoughts. I was only one among many. Infused, uncertain. But now you are no longer quite the self you were . . . I am the only idea that conforms to your being, and you the man that is suited to me . . . I came like a stroke of chance into the working of your head.

p. 31. Your normal intelligence will astonish itself, finding out such paths that you will think yourself mad . . . You will not understand your own perspicacity . . . You will be ashamed of having won so much. You will murmur marvels, in humility.

55

p. 31. Oh, but what a wonder for me, this wretched body, this sickly individuality, this uncertain health ... So many men did not have me.

p. 31. Now we belong to one another. We are confounded one with another, we are in love. You are my Madman-on-account-of-me: YOUR IDEA.

p. 32. My darkness; the hurricane of dreams; thick flock of terrors.

p. 32. My two natures will unite.

p. 32. My dear body, best-beloved form ... in what wedlock did we live before the gift of a foaming mouth made of you this body of death.
But a consecrated virgin, new and iridescent sea-shell, owes to divinity nothing but sacrifice and silence.

p. 33. Alas! laid open to the spirits I have lost my own mystery.

p. 33. She leans in holy expectation, for a new white voice comes from the impure body.

p. 33. Honour of men, sainted Language, discourse prophetic and adorned, fair chains in which the god lost in the flesh is content to be taken, illuminations, bounty! Here speaks a Wisdom, here sounds that august voice which when it sounds knows itself to be no more the voice of a person so much as of the waters and the woods.

p. 35. This quiet roof where doves walk throbs between the pines, between the tombs. There noon in its justice composes out of fires the sea, the sea beginning over and over again for ever.

p. 36. But the giving back of light supposes a desolate half in darkness.

p. 36. Which the Ocean stars with foam torn from the mirrors of the sun.

p. 36. Simple temple to Minerva, mass of calm, visible reserve.

p. 36. And what peace seems to come to birth of itself.

p. 36. Beautiful sky, true sky, look at me who change.
My soul exposed to the torches of the solstice, I bear you, admirable justice.
O for myself alone, to myself alone, within myself.

p. 37. I am the secret alteration in yourself.
My repentances, my doubts, my compulsions are the flaw in your great diamond.

p. 37. Sweet columns, o orchestra of spindles.
We sing at one and the same time as we hold up the skies.
See what candid hymns and what sonority our limpid elements draw from the light.

p. 38. In the sun on my bed after the water, in the sun and in the enormous reflection of the sun on the sea, under my window, and in the reflections and in the reflections of the reflections of the sun and of the suns on the sea in the mirrors, after a bath, coffee, ideas, naked in the sun on my lighted bed, naked, alone, mad–I!

56

p. 39. Break, o my body, this form of thought. Let us run to the water so as to burst from it again fully alive.

p. 39. The blood which burns on lips that yield themselves, the final gifts, the fingers which defend them–all goes beneath the ground and comes back into play again.

p. 40. The real thing that gnaws, the irrefutable worm is not for you who sleep underneath the table; it lives upon life, it is I whom it never leaves.
Love, perhaps, or hatred of myself? Its secret tooth is so close to me that any name could be fitted to it.

p. 43. He who reigns in the Heavens opened the spacious universe with a voice which was the light itself.

p. 43. But the first utterance of his Word: I MYSELF. The proudest of the stars which the mad creator uttered–that am I.

p. 43. Radiant object of my hatred . . . look at yourself in my darkness. Before your ill-omened image, pride of my dark mirror, your uneasiness was so great that your breath upon the clay was a sigh of despair.

p. 44. Tree, great Tree, shadow of Heaven, irresistible Tree of Trees.

p. 44. Her great flank, traversed with gold, fearing neither the sun nor man.

p. 44. The whole Tree of Knowledge shook its great body.

p. 44. But what breathing beneath the darkened breast which the Tree bit with its shadow.

p. 45. The universe is merely a flaw in the purity of Non-Being.

p. 45. As if weary of the pure sight of himself, God broke the obstacle of his perfect eternity; He made himself into the One who dissipates his First Cause in effects, his Unity in stars.

p. 45. I hate the Name which creates so many imperfect wonders.

p. 46. I touch up the heart which trusts itself to it, with a deliberate and mysterious finger.
I disappear into the pure heart. Was there ever so hardened a breast that one could not lodge a dream in it?

p. 46. Soul, said I, sweet dwelling of every forbidden ecstasy, do you sense the sinuous love I have stolen from the Father?
Yield, yield, dear body, to the charms you set before you. Dance, dear body . . . do not think.

p. 46. This charming spot which saw the flesh fall and unite is very dear to me.

p. 46. Against my body, against my soul, against time, against sex and sleep, against life and desire and regret, against knowing and feeling, against myself which I hate as if it were a wife.

p. 47. My satisfaction is an illusion which you will never attain. Is it not the Eternal who created his adversary? Drew him forth from his deliberate foreknowledge? Called him into a garden? Took flesh to know him the better? . . . They have been to the deepest regions of the night . . . They have twined the day that ends to the day that is born by their entwined limbs. They have realized their unity; they have crossed forces; they have breathed one another's breath a long while. None the less they will be unknown to one another for ever.

p. 47. It suffices me that the vast hope of bitter fruit in the air drives mad the children of the slough.

p. 48. Offering to the glory of God the triumph of my sadness.

p. 48. In the heart of the Night, dear Thou who art I, we are one sole being in the heart of the Night.

p. 48. I shall no longer by love resemble other women . . . O God of Gods, there is none but Thou and I . . . I will it with all my strength.

p. 48. That inimitable savour which you find only in yourself.

p. 50. Who weeps there, if it be not the simplicity of the wind, at this hour alone with ultimate diamonds? But who weeps, so near to myself at the moment of weeping?

p. 50. The waves murmur to me a hint of reproach.
I scintillate, in relationship with this unknown sky.

p. 50. Every mortal who does not care to think or to go into things deeply gives a jump at the very mention of my name.

p. 51. Nothing murmured to me that a desire for death could ripen in this clear pulp in the sun.

p. 51. I inquire of my heart what pain keeps it wakeful, what crime consummated by me or upon myself.

p. 51. I was following a serpent which had just bitten me.

p. 51. I was watching myself watching myself.
I keep far from you the clear and sinister mind.

p. 51. A virgin entwined with herself, jealous.
The empty flesh kisses a dark fountain.

p. 51. The mind is not so pure that it never, in idolatry, sets fleeing the walls of its dreary tomb by a solitary access of passion accompanied by the leaping torch-light.
On the golden edge of the universe I think of that longing for death which seizes the Pythoness in whom groans the hope that the world may come to an end.

p. 52. I was the equal and the spouse of day, forming lovingly and with a smile the single support of the beloved and all-powerful height of heaven.

p. 52. 'May my eyes, set in the sky, trace out my temple, and may there rest upon me an unexampled altar!' cried the stone and the pallor of my whole body.

p. 52. My clear clay swam towards my luminous senses . . . Were it not, o Splendour, that at my feet, the Enemy, my shadow . . .

p. 52. I pity us all, whirlwinds of dust that we are.

p. 53. Softly I come: I touch my forehead to this consent . . . This body, I forgive it, a taste of ashes in the mouth.

p. 53. I give myself back wholly to the happiness of descent, laid open to the dark witnesses, with tortured arms, amongst words babbled without end, without myself . . . Abandon yourself alive to the serpents and the spoils. Sleep on! Lower, sleep on! Yet lower . . . sleep, sleep! (The low door is a ring through which the gauze slips. Everything dies away in laughter in the babbling throat. The bird drinks on your lips, but you cannot see . . . Come lower, speak low . . . the dark is not so dark.)

p. 53. Then, o Sun, in spite of myself I am compelled to worship my heart where you take knowledge of yourself, powerful and sweet return of the joy of being born, fire towards which a virgin of flesh and blood uplifts herself beneath the gold mintage of a grateful breast.

BIOGRAPHICAL NOTE

Paul Ambroise Toussaint Jules Valéry was born at Cette (or Sète) on the Mediterranean coast of France in 1871. His father was French, his mother Italian, and he always regarded Italy as his second country. In 1884 the family moved to Montpellier, and it was there that Valéry completed his schooling, which he had found distasteful; he had hoped to join the Navy, but could not reach the standard required in mathematics, an interesting fact in view of his later development. Instead he entered the School of Law at Montpellier in 1889. In 1890, during his year of military service, he met another young writer, Paul Pierre Louÿs, who encouraged him in his literary pursuits, and about the same time he made friends with André Gide. The following year he went to Paris and met Stéphane Mallarmé.

By now he had decided that he would never make a lawyer, and from 1892 to 1896 he led an unsettled existence, partly in London and partly in Paris. In 1896 he entered the War Department in Paris, married in 1900, and in the same year joined the Havas News Agency. He published a few poems in the 1890's, and two prose works, *Introduction à la Méthode de Léonard de Vinci* and *Monsieur Teste*, in 1895 and 1896 respectively, but from then on he published nothing for twenty years, living in retirement and studying with no thought of a literary career. In 1917, however, *La Jeune Parque* appeared, and he was immediately recognized as one of the leading poets of France. From the early 1920's Valéry was a public figure. He was elected a Member of the Académie Française in 1926. In later years his life became that of the eminent man of letters in society: public functions, work for the League of Nations, the steady rise to an international reputation as a great European literary figure. He was in Paris during its occupation by the Germans in the second World War, and died in the year of liberation at the age of seventy-four.

WORKS BY PAUL VALÉRY

This is not an exhaustive list, but gives the principal works. Many of the shorter prose works appeared separately first and were then included in one of the collections such as *Variété*. I have indicated in the text the source of each quotation, but without page numbers since these differ from one edition to another.

POETRY AND POETIC DRAMA

La Jeune Parque, 1917.
Album de Vers Anciens, 1920.
Charmes, 1922.
Amphion, 1931.
Sémiramis, 1934.
Cantate du Narcisse, 1938.
   All these were published by La Nouvelle Révue Française (Gallimard), Paris, and appeared together in:–

Poésies, new and enlarged edition, 1942.

PROSE

All the following were published by La Nouvelle Révue Française (Gallimard), Paris.
Monsieur Teste, 1926; new and enlarged edition, 1946.
Eupalinos, L'Âme et la Danse, 1923; reissued with *Dialogue de l'Arbre*, 1944.
Variété, 1924.
Variété II, 1929.
Variété III, 1936.
Variété IV, 1938.
Variété V, 1944.
L'Idée Fixe, 1932.
Pièces sur l'Art, new and enlarged edition, 1936.
Degas Danse Dessin, 1937.
Mélange, 1941.
Tel Quel I, 1941.
Tel Quel II, 1943.
Mauvaises Pensées et Autres, 1942.
Regards sur le Monde Actuel et autres Essais, new and enlarged edition, 1945.
L'Ange, 1946.
'Mon Faust', 1946.

   The following works are available in English translation:–

Introduction à la Méthode de Léonard de Vinci, translated by T. McGreevy, 1929.
La Soirée avec Monsieur Teste, translated by Merton Gould, 1936.
Eupalinos, translated by W. M. Stewart, 1932.
Le Serpent, translated by Mark Wardle, 1924.
Le Cimetière Marin, translated by C. Day Lewis, 1946.
Regards sur le Monde Actuel, translated by Francis Scarfe, 1951.
L'Âme et la Danse, translated by Dorothy Bussy, 1951.